ROGER TAPPEN'S

Simply Elegant

COOKBOOK

ROGER TAPPEN'S
SIMPLY ELEGANT COOKBOOK

Inquiries should be addressed to:
Benwood Publishing
P.O. Box 993
Chambersburg, PA 17201

Library of Congress Catalog Card # 93-072896

Roger Tappen's Simply Elegant Cookbook

ISBN 0-9638143-0-3

Printed in the United States of America

First Edition

DEDICATION

This book is dedicated to God,
with reverent appreciation for the
blessing of being able to dine at the
bountiful table of life in America.

PREFACE

This cookbook evolves from the first four years of my "Simply Elegant Cooking Classes." It contains the recipes, and much of the instruction, that one would have received had he or she attended every class since 1989.

I have written this book with the same goal in mind that I have when I present my cooking classes. That is to give you simple, down to earth instruction, coupled with available ingredients, that produce elegant recipes which you will be proud to serve.

TABLE OF CONTENTS

fundamentals

GETTING STARTED

Cooking is easy! If it were not, I, and a lot of other people would not be so enthusiastic about the subject.

As you read through the book, and cook through the recipes, it will dawn on you that there is nothing very complicated about the recipes, yet they look and taste great. I have found that applying simple, fundamentally sound techniques to good food produces elegant results.

I enjoy cooking because I know the basic fundamentals. This knowledge keeps me on safe ground in the kitchen. Allow me to share with you my thoughts on what I feel are the basics of successful cooking.

Cooking is the application of heat to food tissue. If we understand cooking methods (the actual application of heat) and we understand the food tissue to which we are applying the heat, we are well on the way to successful cooking. The rest of the journey is aided by knowing how to season food properly, and by knowing when food is cooked to proper completion. That's about it.

I'd like to discuss those areas (food tissue, heating methods, proper seasoning, and knowing when food is done properly) before you enter the recipe section. Learn these fundamentals and you will become an accomplished and confident cook in a very short time.

FOOD TISSUE

Cooking begins with an analysis of the tissue of the items on the menu.

With regards to animal tissue, we must first decide if

the tissue is of the working or non-working variety. To qualify for non-working, animal tissue must come from a skeletal area of the animal that participates little in that animal's common movements.

An example of non-working tissue is the beef tenderloin. The tenderloin lies high on the carcass and between the front shoulder and hind quarters of the beef. The beef moves with motion from the front and hind quarters. The tenderloin just sort of hangs there between the two, going along for the ride.

Because non-working tissue does little work it does not develop tough connecting tissue, and therefore, is tender by nature.

Most of the non-working tissue on mammals is located close to the back bone, midway between the shoulders and the rump of the animal.

This is the area called the loin. It's sometimes referred to as the middle meat.

Another kind of non-working animal tissue is that which is very young. Today's chickens are force fed in confining circumstances and brought to market just a few months after hatching.

Calves are fed special diets and are confined to minimize exercise. Then they are slaughtered while young, producing tender veal cuts. Veal and chicken are examples of young tissue.

Most seafood is tender in the raw state because it has a very high moisture content.

Animal tissue that is of the working variety is that tissue which comes from an area on the carcass that is involved with the work or main motions of the particular animal. The older the animal, the more work it has done — so more tough tissue has developed.

In mammals, the bulk of the working tissue is located in the front shoulders, the upper hind quarters, and the legs.

Vegetable tissue can be quickly analyzed by feel or bite.

We judge vegetable tissue with regards to density and moisture content.

A carrot is dense, whereas a mushroom is less dense and contains a great deal of moisture.

Working and non-working animal tissue, and high and low density vegetable tissue require different cooking methods.

COOKING METHODS - APPLYING THE HEAT

There are many cooking methods, but they all can be separated into just two basic categories. There are moist cooking methods, and dry cooking methods.

Use moist cooking methods to cook working tissue from animals, and the most dense vegetable tissues. Moist cooking usually involves low to medium heat settings, and cooking times of long duration.

Water or steam is involved and the food is usually covered. Water used in moist heat cooking methods may be in the form of broths, juice, wine, or other seasoned liquids. The common trait in these liquids is that they can produce steam or, when used in volume, the food is submerged.

Examples of moist heat cooking methods are blanching, boiling, poaching, steaming, simmering, stewing, and braising.

Use dry heat cooking styles to prepare tissue that is young, non-working, has a high moisture content, or has low density - boneless chicken breasts, fish fillets, beef from the loin, pork tenderloin, shrimp, scallops, mushrooms, or zucchini. Dry heat usually means high heat. Fats or oils are used in varying amounts. Foods are not covered and cooking times are of short duration, unless a large mass of food is involved.

Examples of dry heat cooking methods are baking and roasting, broiling, pan broiling, outdoor grilling, sautéing, stir frying, pan frying, and deep frying. Deep frying does not seem like a dry method. It qualifies because of the high temperature used and because hot oil, not water, is the heating agent.

Some foods may be cooked with either dry or moist cooking styles. Potatoes may be baked or boiled. The same is true of chicken parts. Deciding which method to use depends on the desired outcome. A beef steak from the loin would have little plate appearance if it was boiled. We would miss that darkened surface appearance and the flavor that results from high heat crisping the fats, sugars, and juices of the meat.

So when you first analyze your menu, decide the nature of the tissues involved. Then match each tissue with a cooking method that best takes you to your desired result, high and dry, or slow and moist.

SEASONING FOOD

When cooking foods that require medium to long cooking times season the food in stages. Season moderately at the start. Taste and correct seasonings at the cooking midpoint. Taste and adjust again twenty minutes before serving.

Herbs and spices have less effect on recipes after the seasonings cook for a while. An example: If you took three bites from the same onion — one when raw, another after the onion had been simmered for 30 minutes, and the last bite after the onion cooked for two hours, each bite would be progressively milder. That's what happens to your spices in soups, stews, sauces, or any seasoned dish that cooks for a long time. Adding more spice along the way gives the recipe its true intended flavor through the addition of fresh seasonings. Adding spices or herbs near the completion of the recipe brings the flavor to a peak. You may not notice, but arriving guests or family members that enter the room will enjoy an enhanced aroma that the added spices helped to create.

Spicing foods that cook quickly is best done moderately. It is difficult to remove the spice effect if it is over-done. In most cases seasonings can be added very easily as the food is being tasted.

To become familiar with spices and herbs, taste them. Place some in your hand. Smell them at close range. Then taste a small amount. Imagine that taste with the food

groups (vegetables, beef, pork, chicken, seafood).

Store your spices and herbs in tightly sealed jars in areas of moderate temperature. Keep them out of direct sunlight.

Unless you are involved with volume cooking, purchase your spices in the smallest amounts possible. This forces rotation and results in fresh supplies on hand. If two chefs cook the same recipe, season it in stages, and present it at the same time, the cook using the old spices will not be able to match the flavor of the chef using fresh spices.

Wines are wonderful seasonings. Again, become familiar with these liquid seasonings by tasting them. Avoid using wines in your food that you would not serve a guest in a glass. Wines can easily dominate the flavor of recipes. Use them in moderation. Use the season, stir, and taste method. Wines affect the recipe's flavor in seconds. That is why the season and taste method works very well when using wines with food.

It is easy to over-pour wines, especially when the bottles are full. I like to use an easy to control, inserted, pour-top on my cooking wines. Lacking a pour-top , I'll pour a little in a small cup. Then I'll season the recipe from the cup.

KNOWING WHEN FOODS ARE DONE CORRECTLY

Everything has gone right until now. We have chosen an appropriate cooking method to match the food tissue of an entree we wish to serve. We have seasoned it properly. Our last important task is to serve it when it is at its peak with regards to flavor and texture to bite and chew.

Fortunately there are some guidelines to help us.

White fleshed seafood (whitefish, crabs, lobster, scallops, shrimp) is done as soon as it is white throughout. With shrimp and scallops cut a large one in half. If it is pure white, the whole batch is one. They both cook quickly, so test as you cook to avoid overcooking.

Cut into the thick areas of fish fillets and scallops with a sharp knife. Twist the knife and inspect the flesh. If it is white it is done. The rule — ten minutes cooking time per inch of flesh in preheated oven or broiler — works well with fish and lobster.

Clams and oysters are done when their shells open. Discard those in the batch which do not open.

To know when a kettle of steamed crabs are done, break off and taste a claw from a large crab near the top. If it is done, the batch is done.

Seafood, in general, cooks quickly. Remember its tissue has a high moisture content. Heat travels very efficiently through moisture. Seafood suffers greatly when overcooked. Test it as it cooks to avoid this dilemma.

Meats can be checked for cooking completion by measuring their internal temperature. Use the incredibly handy instant reading thermometer for this purpose. These thermometers are not left in the meat as it cooks, but rather inserted into the middle of the flesh, away from bone, near the estimated end of the cook time. They work with roasts, steaks, chops, poultry, and even ground meats.

People prefer beef done in varying degrees. Beef is rare at 135 degrees, medium at 150 degrees, and well done at 170 degrees.

A precooked smoked ham is ready to serve when it reaches about 140 degrees in the center.

Chicken, game hen, duck, geese, and turkey are ready to serve when the meat thermometer reaches 180 degrees.

Check the thigh and the breast areas. Remember to avoid touching bone with the probe of the thermometer.

Put the pork on the table when it reaches 170 degrees.

Lamb is just done at 170 degrees, and well done at 180 degrees.

If you know someone who enjoys cooking but does not have an instant reading food thermometer, it would be a perfect gift. If that person is yourself, all the better. Purchase the variety that reads from 0 to 220 degrees.

To test vegetable tissue for correct cooking, bite it, or pierce it with a sharp probe. A metal skewer works well. Undercook your vegetables a little to retain color, texture, flavor, and nutrients. Taste as you cook to avoid overcooking. Arrest the cooking process with cold water, in colanders, under the faucet.

Use the fundamentals discussed in this section and cooking will become a pleasant and rewarding activity. Successful cooking always results when you do the following:

Apply the proper cooking method to the tissue being cooked.

Season foods moderately at the beginning, and taste them as they cook. Adjust seasonings while the food cooks, and again before serving.

Serve food at its peak of flavor and texture by checking internal temperature and color, or by tasting for flavor and texture.

Appetizers

STUFFED STRAWBERRIES

14 - 16 nicely shaped large strawberries
1 container (8 ounces) Philadelphia Brand Strawberry Flavored Creamed Cheese

Rinse strawberries under cold running water and allow them to dry on paper towels.

Cap each berry by cutting a thin layer of fruit off the top along with the green leaf top. Set the tops aside. Slice a small piece off the tip of each berry in such a way that the strawberry will balance and stand upright.

Using the small end of a mellon baller, cut a circular cavity in the flattened top of the strawberries. Discard the fruit pulp from this area.

Allow the chilled Strawberry Flavored Cream Cheese to set at room temperature, opened, for twenty minutes. Place it in a pastry bag fitted with a small fluted tip. Pipe the cream cheese into the cavity cut in each berry. Fill in a circular motion and finish with a "soft ice cream top" peak.

You may also use the rounded back (tip) of a standard teaspoon to fill strawberries.

Arrange the filled strawberries in circular fashion around a plate of contrasting color. Fill in the space on the plate with the cut berry tops, cut side down and with green stem showing.

BEEF TERIYAKI BITES

1 pound beef tenderloin
¼ cup sherry
¼ cup honey
¼ cup soy sauce
30 - 5 inch bamboo skewers

Cut tenderloin into ¼ inch slices. Cut those slices into 1 inch square pieces. Makes about 90 pieces.

In a deep bowl stir together the sherry, honey, and soy sauce.

Add the cut pieces of meat and stir to coat with the marinade. Cover with plastic wrap and marinate for about an hour at room temperature, or for several hours in refrigeration. Stir occasionally.

On each skewer thread 3 pieces of meat. Skewer the meat from corner to corner so that the pieces of meat are aligned in 3 consecutive diamond shapes. Place 6 skewers on a microwave friendly plate. Cook at high setting for 1½ to 2 minutes. Rotate the plate halfway through cooking time. Repeat with other skewers.

SWEET & SOUR MEATBALLS

1 pound ground chuck
¾ cup minced onion
1 egg - beaten
½ cup fresh minced parsley
⅓ cup water
¼ cup dry bread crumbs
1 teaspoon each - salt, oregano, thyme, and pepper
1 bottle (4 ounces) Kitchen Bouquet
½ cup ketchup
¼ cup light molasses
¼ cup Dijon style mustard

Mix the ketchup, light molasses, and Dijon mustard in a microwave-safe bowl. Cook on medium for 4 minutes. Stir after each 2 minutes. Place the sauce in a warming appliance.

Combine first 10 ingredients in a bowl. Roll the mixture into 30-35 bite-sized meatballs. Pour a few tablespoons of Kitchen Bouquet into a shallow dish and thin it a bit with water. Coat 8-10 meatballs with the dark mixture and place them on a microwave-safe plate. Cook on medium high for 2 minutes. Rotate the plate after 1 minute. Check for doneness and place the meatballs in the sauce. Cook the meatballs in batches until all are done. Serve with toothpicks.

LIVERWURST & ONION PÂTÉ

1 pound liverwurst or braunsweiger
¾ cup finely minced onion
1½ tablespoons fresh mince parsley
Approximately ½ of a 5 ounce bottle of A-1 Sauce (or to taste)

Fit your food processor with the standard cut and mix blade. Cut the liverwurst into about six equal-sized pieces. Put the liverwurst, the finely chopped onion, the minced parsley, and a few tablespoons of A-1 sauce in the processor and mix the ingredients using the pulse button. Stop to scrape down the sides of the chamber if needed for even mixing.

Taste the mixture for seasoning adjustment. Try to achieve a texture that will stand on a plate on its own and that is still spreadable. More A-1 sauce may be needed. If you are happy with the taste, a little water can be used to thin the pâté.

Butter the inside surfaces of some measuring cups, small bowls, or other uniformly shaped containers and press your pâté into these containers. you may refrigerate them, or if you are to use them soon you may leave them at room temperature. Tap the pâtés onto a serving plate and surround with toast points, pumpernickel or rye cocktail bread, or variety crackers. Garnish with endive and cherry tomatoes for color. Be sure to provide a spreading knife.

CHICKEN BREAST & GREEN ONION APPETIZER

For 12 appetizers assemble:

3 raw, skinned, boneless chicken breast halves
3 thick stemmed green onions
Golden Dipt brand chicken coating
2 tablespoons butter
1½ cups vegetable oil
toothpicks

Cut the raw chicken breast halves into approximately 1-inch pieces. Dry them with paper towels and lay them on waxed paper. Sprinkle with salt and pepper and dredge them with Golden Dipt chicken coating.

Heat the oil in skillet to medium-high. When hot, fry the coated breast pieces. Turn them often for even browning and doneness. They should be done in 8 to 10 minutes. Drain them on paper towels.

While the breast pieces are frying, cut the green onions into 1 inch pieces. Sauté them in the butter for about 3 minutes. The butter is more for seasoning than cooking. Remove them from the hot butter while they are still crisp.

As soon as onion pieces and chicken breasts are cool enough to handle, skewer one piece of chicken breast and one piece of green onion on a toothpick. Repeat until ingredients are all used. Serve warm on a heated platter.

CHICKEN LIVER BROCHETTES

6 chicken livers per guest served
3 strips of bacon per 6 chicken livers
2 green onions per 6 chicken livers
flour for dredging
2 tablespoons butter
salt & pepper

Wash chicken livers and trim any excess fat. Salt and pepper chicken livers. Brown them in melted butter and set them aside on paper towels.

Fry bacon until about ¾ cooked.

While bacon is frying cut green onions into 1 ½ -inch pieces. Sauté in 2 tablespoons butter for about 3 minutes. Remove from pan an drain on paper towels.

Blot partially cooked bacon on paper towels.

Skewer a piece of green onion. Cut a piece of bacon in half and wrap a half bacon strip around a chicken liver.

Skewer the wrapped chicken liver next to the first piece of green onion. Skewer another piece of green onion. Wrap another chicken liver with bacon and add it to the skewer. Finish the skewer with another piece of green onion. Repeat this process until you have enough appetizers for the intended number of guests. One appetizer will be 3 pieces of green onion and two bacon wrapped chicken livers. For a smaller appetizer use one bacon wrapped chicken liver with a piece of green onion skewered above and below on a small skewer or toothpick.

Bake a 375 degrees for about 12-15 minutes. Turn once after about 7 minutes. Drain on paper towels. Serve warm or hot.

CHICKEN NACHOS

4 boneless chicken breast halves
1 package (8 ounces) cream cheese
½ cup sour cream
minced jalapena peppers or green chilies to taste
2 teaspoons cumin
1 can (16 ounces) enchilada sauce
2½ cup grated cojack cheese
1 package nacho chips

In a wide skillet pour water to cover the chicken breasts and bring to a boil over high heat. Reduce heat to a simmer and poach the chicken for about 10 minutes, or until just done. Turn the meat once. Set the meat aside to cool.

Allow the cream cheese to come to room temperature. Place it in a large bowl with the sour cream, cumin, and peppers or chilies. Stir to blend.

Cut the chicken into bite-sized pieces and fold into the cream cheese mixture.

Place a dollop of the chicken mixture on each of several nacho chips. Spoon a bit of enchilada sauce on top of each dollop of chicken mixture. Top the chicken and sauce with a sprinkling of grated cojack cheese.

Place the nachos in a 325 degree oven, or microwave, until the cheese is melted and the chicken is heated through.

Makes about 30 appetizers.

JAPANESE STYLE SKEWERED CHICKEN

6 boneless, skinless chicken breast halves
6 green onions
¾ cup all purpose flour
½ teaspoon salt
½ cup ice water
1 beaten egg
oriental five spice powder
vegetable oil for deep fat frying
Kikkoman soy sauce
sweet mustard

Cut breast halves into 1¼-inch by 1¼ -inch pieces. Cut green onions into 1-inch lengths. On short bamboo skewers alternate pieces of chicken and green onion. Season the skewered chicken and green onion with a liberal amount of five spice powder.

Use a pie pan or shallow dish to prepare the batter. Start by mixing the salt and flour. Beat the egg and then combine it with the ice water. Mix the egg and water thoroughly. Add the egg mixture to the flour all at once. Stir until all the flour is moistened and a thick batter is created.

Dip the skewers in the batter and turn and swirl them

until well-coated. Carefully place the skewers in hot deep fat. Fry about 5 minutes or until the chicken is medium brown. Drain on paper towels.

Serve with a dipping sauce of 2 parts sweet mustard and 1 part Kikkoman soy sauce.

CHICKEN TENDERS IN CAJUN MARINADE

18 chicken breast tenderloins, about 1½ pounds
¼ pound butter or margarine
¼ cup white chablis wine
½ teaspoon onion powder
½ teaspoon garlic powder
½ teaspoon ground white pepper
½ teaspoon ground red pepper
½ teaspoon ground black pepper
½ teaspoon dried thyme

Melt butter in a sauce pan over medium heat. Add the chablis, onion powder, garlic powder, white pepper, red pepper,black pepper, and thyme. Stir and simmer for about 10 minutes.

Marinate the chicken tenders in a zip lock bag or large bowl containing the cooled sauce. Marinate for 40 minutes at room temperature or for a few hours under refrigeration.

Cook the marinaded tenders on a grill, under the broiler, or in a sauté pan with a little of the marinade.

Makes 18 appetizers.

■ Buy spices in the smallest available containers. This encourages rotation and ensures freshness.

SWEET & SOUR CHICKEN WINGS

5 pounds chicken wings or drumettes
4 eggs, beaten
2 cups corn starch
1 teaspoon garlic salt
1 teaspoon black pepper
1 teaspoon salt
vegetable oil for frying

Cut each wing into 3 pieces at the joints. Discard the tips (third, and smallest section) or use them for making stock. Dip the other chicken pieces in the beaten eggs. Roll them in the corn starch and coat them all over. Fry them in a skillet of heated vegetable oil until golden.

Remove the chicken pieces to a shallow baking dish.

Make a seasoning mix using the garlic powder, black pepper, and salt. Sprinkle this mixture evenly over the chicken. Turn and repeat.

Make a sauce using the following ingredients:

½ cup chicken broth
1 cup sugar
1 cup cider vinegar
6 tablespoons ketchup
2 tablespoons Kikkoman soy sauce
2 teaspoons salt

You can mix this sauce in a bowl with a whisk. Don't cook the sauce. Pour the sauce over the chicken in the baking dish. Bake 30 minutes at 350, uncovered. Turn once after 15 minutes.

PORK & GARLIC WON TONS

½ pound lean ground pork
½ teaspoon garlic powder
3 green onions - chopped fine
1 medium-sized carrot - grated fine
1 egg - beaten
1 package won ton skins

Mix the ground pork, garlic powder, chopped green onions, grated carrot, and egg in a bowl. Mix thoroughly to affect a proper seasoning.

Set up a production line on your counter — pork mixture, cup of water, and won ton skins. Lay a single won ton wrapper on the counter. Place a heaped teaspoon of pork mixture in the center of the skin. Moisten two adjacent edges of the skin with your moistened finger tips. Fold the wrap so that the two dry edges rest on, and are aligned with the two moist edges. The skin is now in the shape of a triangle. Press the edges together with the tines of a fork to seal.

Repeat until the pork mixture is gone (about 18-20 won tons).

Lay the prepared won tons on wax paper that is sprinkled with a little cornmeal.

Fry the won tons in enough hot oil to cover until golden brown. Turn the won tons as they cook. Fry four or five at a time for about 5 minutes per batch.

Serve with teriyaki sauce or plain Kikkoman soy sauce for dipping.

PORK & GREEN ONION APPETIZER

1 raw, trimmed, pork tenderloin (pork fish)
2 bunches medium thick green onions
1 bottle Kikkoman teriyaki sauce
toothpicks soaked in water (optional)

Trim the pork tenderloin of all external fat tissue. Slice the tenderloin thinly at a right angle to produce several coin-like pieces of pork.

Cut the green onions into lengths equaling the diameter of the pork "coins". Discard the root ends. Cut and save the tops for other uses (soups, stuffing, etc.).

Wrap each piece of green onion with a piece of pork. Secure with a toothpick. Place the "saddled" green onion pieces in a shallow pan containing the teriyaki sauce. Marinate them at room temperature for 30 minutes or more. Turn at least once during marinade.

When ready to cook place them under the broiler for about 8 minutes or until pork is cooked. Turn at mid-point of cooking time. Serve hot or warm.

These appetizers can be skewered to well-drained chunks of pineapple either before or after cooking.

PORK TENDERLOIN TERIYAKI

1 pork fish
1 cup teriyaki sauce
bamboo skewer

This recipe can be used as an appetizer or as an entree. Simply double the amounts above to serve four people as a main dish.

Trim the pork fish to bare meat. Cut it across its length

at 1 inch intervals. Spray your meat mallet with Pam and pound each pork round into a thin cutlet. For appetizers, cut the longest of the cutlets in half.

Place the teriyaki sauce and pork cutlets in a zip lock bag and marinate 30 minutes at room temperature, or more than an hour in refrigeration.

Soaking the bamboo skewers in warm water for 20 to 30 minutes will prevent them from burning on the grill.

Skewer the cutlets, lengthwise, and cook them over hot coals for 3 minutes per side. Serve with extra teriyaki sauce for passing around the table.

Kikkoman brands makes an excellent teriyaki sauce. Or you may make your own.

Simple syrup is made by stirring sugar into boiling water. A one to one ratio, or equal parts sugar and water, are used.

Teriyaki Sauce

½ cup simple syrup
½ cup Kikkoman soy sauce
1 cup chicken broth
½ teaspoon powdered ginger
¼ teaspoon garlic powder
cornstarch

(In order to adjust this sauce to taste, have extra simple syrup, soy sauce, and chicken broth on hand.)

Combine the first 5 ingredients in a sauce pan. Bring to a low boil. Combine 1 tablespoon cornstarch with 2 tablespoons cold water and stir to affect a smooth mix. Add the cornstarch mixture to the teriyaki sauce and stir to thicken. Adjust flavors to your liking.

CRUNCHY COCKTAIL FRANKS

1 pound hot dogs or 1 package cocktail franks
1 bottle (28 ounces) ketchup
2 cups corn flakes crumbs

Cut hot dogs into bite sized pieces. Microwave on medium high for 1 ½ minutes. Blot on paper towels.

Pour about a cup of ketchup in a pie pan (or similar low pan).

Place 1 cup corn flake crumbs in another pie pan. Roll the cooked hot dog pieces in the ketchup, and then in the corn flake crumbs. Serve on toothpicks. Add ketchup and corn flake crumbs to the respective pans as needed. Makes 30-40 crunchy appetizers.

CRAB & CHEESE MUFFINS

6 English muffins, split in half
12 ounces shelled crab meat
1 jar (8 ounces) Kraft Old English Cheese
¼ pound margarine or butter
1½ tablespoons Miracle Whip
¼ teaspoon garlic powder
¼ teaspoon seasoned salt

Allow all ingredients but crab meat to come to room temperature. Blend ingredients together in a bowl. Fold in the crab meat until thoroughly mixed. Spread on the English muffin halves.

Heat in a hot oven or under the broiler until bubbly. Cut muffins into quarters for bite sized appetizers.

■ All crab meat sold in stores and seafood markets,

unless still in the possession of a live crab, is cooked. Gently check it for shell fragments with your finger tips. Then it's ready to use. Avoid overcooking crab meat recipes.

SHRIMP ON THE BARBE

24 large thawed shrimp
6 tablespoons butter
3 tablespoons lime juice
3 large cloves garlic - minced
6 tablespoons bottled chili sauce
4 tablespoons Herlocher's dipping mustard
dried minced chives

Melt butter over low heat. When melted add the lime juice and minced garlic. Cook 3 minutes and remove from the heat.

While the butter is melting, peel and devein the shrimp. Place the peeled shrimp in the lime butter.

Mix the chili sauce and the dipping mustard in a small bowl.

Either skewer the shrimp or use a grilltopper to cook the shrimp on the grill. If thin round skewers are used, it is helpful to thread the shrimp with two skewers set ½-inch apart. This prevents the shrimp from spinning on the skewer and makes them generally easier to handle. Soak wooden skewers in warm water for 20-30 minutes prior to using.Place the shrimp on the grill and immediately brush them with the chili-mustard sauce. Brush them at least twice in a 5-minute cooking period. Turn the shrimp often.

Shrimp are very easy to overcook on a hot grill. They become tough when overcooked. Even a minute too long is noticeable in a negative manner. Cook the shrimp until they are well-curled (on a grilltopper), or until they are bright pink and firm (but not hard) to the touch. When in doubt taste a large one. If it is done, they are all done.

Just before serving sprinkle some chopped chives over the grilled shrimp. Serve with chili-mustard sauce for dipping.

SHRIMP DIP

8 ounces cream cheese (room temperature)
⅔ cup Miracle Whip
3 tablespoons bottled chili sauce
2 tablespoons minced onion
1 or 2, 6-ounce cans medium shrimp
salt & pepper to taste

Drain canned shrimp and pat dry on paper towels. Set aside. Fold remaining ingredients together in a bowl. Add the shrimp and mix in gently. Cover and refrigerate for about an hour. Serve with variety crackers.

CREAM CHEESE, KIKKOMAN & SESAME SEEDS

1 brick (8 ounces) cream cheese
small container sesame seeds
Kikkoman soy sauce, Triscuit crackers

Unwrap cream cheese and place it on a dinner-sized plate in brick form. Allow it to come to room temperature. Toast sesame seeds in a dry skillet over medium heat. Stir or shake pan occasionally. When sesame seeds brown cover the brick of cream cheese with 4 - 6 tablespoons of Kikkoman soy sauce. Top the cream cheese and Kikkoman with the toasted sesame seeds. Serve with Triscuit crackers.

CHEESE & RYE HORS D'OEUVRES

6 ounces sharp yellow cheddar cheese (shredded)
5 slices cooked bacon
½ cup chopped raw onion
Miracle Whip (to taste)
party rye and pumpernickel breads

Use the food processor to break up the bacon. Use pulse button. Bacon should be coarsely crumbled, not fine. Add chopped onion. Pulse the machine again. Add the shredded cheddar cheese and Miracle Whip and pulse until a cheese spread consistency is reached. Taste for seasoning adjustment.

Spread on party rye or pumpernickel bread and broil until melted. Serve hot.

Makes enough cheese and bacon spread for 30 party rye appetizers.

DEVILED EGGS

Here are some basics and some new ideas for an old favorite appetizer:

Use eggs for hard boiling that have been around for a while – 5 days or more. The longer eggs sit around the more air seeps between the thin outer membrane and the shell. When this occurs they become much easier to peel.

Start with cold water to cover however many eggs you intend to boil. Bring rapidly to a boil, uncovered. Boil 3 to 4 minutes. Remove from heat and cover. Let set covered 12 minutes. Drain hot water and cool with cold water.

To shell hard-cooked eggs crack all around on a hard flat surface. Gently roll them between your palms to further loosen shell. Begin peeling at the large end.

To center yolks in hard-boiled eggs crowd them in a small sauce pan so that they are standing on end. Large end down with thin end up is best, but to get all the eggs to support each other in a vertical manner you may need to alternate a few eggs with small ends down.

Basic Deviled Egg recipe — For 6 eggs use ¼ cup mayonnaise or Miracle Whip, 1 teaspoon vinegar, 1 teaspoon prepared mustard, ¼ teaspoon salt, and dash pepper. Halve eggs lengthwise; remove yolks and mash with aforementioned ingredients. Mix well and refill egg whites.

Additions to standard filling can include: horseradish, anchovies, parsley, chopped onions or chives, flaked seafood, chopped black or green olives, or crumbled crisp bacon. To display finished deviled eggs cover a serving platter with green leaf lettuce leaves, or endive, and place eggs around platter. Greens will help support eggs and keep them from rolling. The greens also provide a nice color contrast. Alfalfa sprouts also make a great nest for deviled eggs.

Deviled eggs are attractive when they are garnished with a sprinkling of paprika, crumbled bacon, red or black caviar, bits of pimento, sliced green or black olives, minced green herbs such as parsley, chives, basil or green onion, or bits of smoked ham.

Deviled eggs can be prepared up to six hours ahead of the serving time. Be sure to cover snugly with plastic wrap and refrigerate until 30 minutes before serving.

FRUIT KABOBS & VANILLA MINT YOGURT SAUCE

1 cup plain yogurt
2 teaspoons sugar
⅛ teaspoon vanilla
2 tablespoons minced mint leaves
1 pineapple, peeled, cored, and cubed
3 kiwi fruits, peeled and sliced
2 pints strawberries, hulled
1 honeydew melon, peeled and cubed
into 24 6-inch cubes

In a bowl whisk together the yogurt, sugar, vanilla, and the mint. Fresh mint leaves can occasionally be found in local produce departments. Dried mint leaves are usually stocked in the spice section on the grocery shelves. (The sauce may be made a day ahead and kept covered and chilled.)

Skewer the fruits, alternating the pineapple, kiwi, strawberries, and honeydew melon pieces.

Serve with yogurt sauce.

Makes about 24 fruit kabobs.

ORANGE BOWL FRUIT CUP

1 large orange per 2 guests served
white sugar for marinating fruit
various colorful fruit of the season
1 bunch endive for garnish

Select colorful fruits such as skinned kiwi, red, black, and white grapes, mandarin oranges, maraschino cherries, peaches, pears, etc. You may serve the fruits with no preparation other than cutting and cubing by using a sweet dressing at the time of serving. Or you can add a few tablespoons of white sugar to the fruit mix. Stir in the sugar gently. Cover the bowl and refrigerate for several hours. Stir again occasionally.

With your thumb and index finger, hold an orange on a counter with the stem and blossom ends parallel to the counter. Beginning at the center, midway between thumb and fingertip, pierce the orange with your paring knife on a 45-degree angle (/). The cut should be perpendicular to the counter and pass a little more than halfway through the orange. Make another, equally deep, vertical cut on an opposite 45-degree angle (\). Continue cutting a series of (/\) cuts (/\/\/\/\/\) around the center line circumference of the orange. Continue cutting around the center of the orange until your last cut reaches your first cut.

You can now pull the orange apart. Using a curved instrument like a grapefruit knife, remove the pulp from the orange peel. Fill the hollow orange peel with the fruit salad mixture. If you have sugared the fruit and allowed it to stand you can serve it in the orange cup with its own juices. If you are using fresh raw fruit, dress it with Poppy seed dressing. Set each orange cup in a ring of endive on a saucer or small plate.

BREAD STICKS WITH HERBAL BUTTER

¼ pound butter - room temperature
¼ teaspoon garlic powder
⅛ teaspoon cracked black pepper
⅛ teaspoon thyme
1 teaspoon fresh minced parsley
1 teaspoon finely minced green onion tops
24 cooked bread sticks

Place room temperature butter in a mixing bowl. Add spices and stir well. Cover and allow mixture to blend 1 hour at room temperature or 3 hours under refrigeration.

There are almost as many variations to herbal butters as there are spices. Don't forget the liquid spices. Tabasco, Worcestershire sauce, soy sauce, etc. I urge you to experiment and use herbal butters on fish, fowl, red meat, vegetables and bread and rolls.

Brush cooked bread sticks, rolls or bread with the herbal butter of your choice. Wrap them in foil and heat in a 325 degree oven, or over medium grill for 20 minutes. Serve warm.

QUICHE LORRAINE

12 ounces, bacon
1 unbaked 9-inch pie shell
4 eggs
1½ cups heavy cream
½ teaspoon salt
¼ teaspoon pepper
pinch nutmeg
⅓ cup grated Swiss cheese

Cut bacon into 1-inch pieces and cook until crisp. Drain on paper towels. Spread the cooked bacon over the bottom of the pie shell.

Beat the three eggs in a bowl. Beat the eggs vigorously with a whisk or with an electric mixer until they become frothy. Add cream, seasonings, and grated cheese. Stir just enough to blend. Pour mixture into pie shell and bake uncovered in a 375 degree oven until the filling is firm and the top is nicely browned. Allow quiche to rest at room temperature for 15 minutes before slicing.

■ Crack raw eggs on flat surfaces (like a counter top), and not on sharp edges (like the rim of a pan). Shell pieces will tend to be larger if the egg is cracked on a flat surface and will be much easier to retrieve from the mixture into which you drop the egg.

SANGRIA

1 - 750 milliliter bottle dry red, or rosé wine
2 cups carbonated water
2 oranges
1 lemon
1 lime
⅓ cup sugar

Chill wine and carbonated water. Cut 1 orange, ½ lemon and ½ lime into slices. Squeeze juice from remaining fruit into a pitcher; stir in sugar. Stir in wine; add carbonated water and fruit slices.

Serve in wine glasses.

Makes 8 - 6 ounce servings.

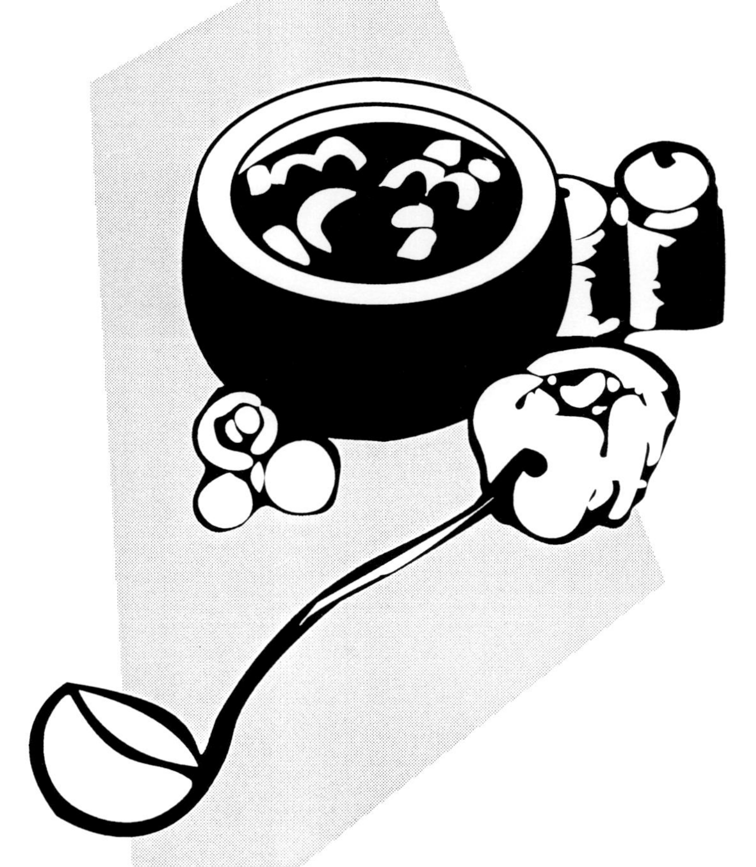

Soups

TACO SOUP

1½ pounds ground beef (chuck)
1 tablespoon cumin
2 teaspoons chili powder
1 teaspoon garlic powder
½ teaspoon basil
1 tablespoon minced fresh parsley
¾ cup chopped green pepper
1 can (28 ounces) whole tomatoes - crushed
1 can (15 ounces) tomato sauce
1 - 10 ¾ ounce can tomato soup
2 - 15 ounce cans kidney beans
1 tablespoon brown sugar
10 ounces cojack cheese - grated
1 package (11 ounces) Dorito nacho-flavored tortilla chips
water

Brown the ground chuck in a stock pot large enough to hold a gallon of soup. Season the meat as it cooks with the cumin, chili powder, and garlic powder. After about 5 minutes, and before the meat is browned, add the chopped peppers and onions. Continue cooking and stirring the meat until it is browned.

Add the tomato sauce and half a can of water. Add the tomato soup and a full can of water. Stir and cook over medium high heat.

Add the crushed tomatoes and the kidney beans (drained). Add the basil, parsley, and the brown sugar.

Bring the soup to a simmer and cook for about an hour. Stir from the bottom occasionally. Skim any floating fat off the surface of the soup with a ladle. Taste and correct seasonings after 30 minutes, and again just before serving. The soup should taste like a sweet chili.

When serving the soup in bowls, top each serving with grated cojack cheese and coarsely crushed Doritos.

Serves 6 to 8 as an entree soup — more as an appetizer soup.

ITALIAN WEDDING SOUP

¾ pound ground chuck
1 tablespoon fresh mined parsley
½ teaspoon each - garlic powder, basil, oregano
1½ tablespoon grated parmesan cheese
¼ cup dried bread crumbs
1 small beaten egg
2 tablespoons butter
8 cups chicken broth
escarole - 1 small head
1 grated carrot
1 tablespoon fresh minced parsley
3 tablespoons minced onion
3 tablespoons minced celery
3 or 4 pieces stale white bread
2 or 4 beaten eggs
3 tablespoons melted butter
parmesan cheese to pass at table

Combine the ground chuck, 1 tablespoon parsley, garlic powder, basil, oregano, 1½ tablespoons parmesan cheese, bread crumbs, and beaten egg in a bowl and mix well with your hands. Roll the mixture into bite-sized meatballs.

Brown the meatballs in butter. Drain off excess fat and set aside.

Heat the chicken broth to a low boil and stir in the grated carrot, minced onion and celery, and the second tablespoon of minced parsley. Wash and dry the escarole. Chop it into bite-sized pieces and add it to the broth. Add the browned meatballs. Simmer the soup about 15 minutes before serving.

While the soup simmers prepare the egged croutons. Cut the stale bread into bite-sized pieces. Stir them in the beaten egg to coat them. Fry them in 3 tablespoons melted butter until the egg sets. Keep them warm. Serve the egged croutons on top of individual servings of soup.

Put a bowl of grated parmesan cheese on your table when you serve the soup.

Serves 6 to 8.

HAM-BEAN SOUP

2 large or 3 medium smoked ham hocks
⅓ cup bacon fat
1 cup chopped onion
2 cups chopped celery
2 medium carrots - grated fine
1 can (28 ounces) peeled tomatoes - crushed
4 cans (15 ounces each) great northern beans
2 tablespoons brown sugar
1 small whole onion stuck with 4 cloves
⅓ cup ketchup
2 cups Bisquick baking mix
4 quarts water

Heat ⅓ cup bacon fat in a wide skillet over medium heat. Slice the ham hocks, deeply and about an inch apart, top to bottom, about 5 times. Fry the hocks in the hot oil for about 20 minutes. Turn them often. Remove the hocks and allow them to cool.

After removing the hocks deglaze the pan by carefully adding a cup of warm water to the hot fat. Stir and scrape the pan bottom to incorporate any solid bits that stick to the pan. Add the celery and onions and sauté them for 5 minutes. This mixture of deglazed pan liquid and sautéed vegetables is the foundation for a tasty ham broth that will be the dominant flavor factor in ham-bean soup. Transfer this mixture to a large soup pan.

Add the 4 quarts water to the mixture in the new pot. Add the crushed tomatoes, shredded carrot, the onion and cloves, half of the brown sugar, and half of the ketchup. Mash the contents of one of the cans of beans in a bowl to make a moist paste. Add the crushed beans and the other 3 cans (beans intact) to the stock.

Add the ham hocks to the soup and bring the pot to a simmer. Allow the soup to simmer uncovered for about an hour. Remove the hocks from the soup and allow them to cool. While the hocks cool place the Bisquick in a bowl and add about 1½ cups soup broth. Stir to affect a moist paste. Add this back to the soup pot and stir thoroughly. After the soup thickens you may adjust the consistency of the soup with water.

Carefully trim the meat from the cooled ham hocks. Cut it into small pieces and add it back to the soup. Season to taste with the remaining brown sugar and ketchup. Remove the onion and cloves before serving. Makes about 1½ gallons.

KOREAN CHICKEN CORN SOUP

2 quarts chicken broth
2 cups minced cooked chicken
½ cup minced cooked ham
2 egg whites, lightly beaten
1 can (1 pound) cream style corn
½ cup chopped green onion tops
1 teaspoon sesame oil
salt & pepper to taste
cornstarch for thickening (optional)

Bring chicken broth to a boil. Add chicken, ham, green onion, salt & pepper, sesame oil, and stir. Return to a boil. Add beaten egg whites and stir with a whisk. Stir in one direction. Lastly, add the cream style corn. Stir again and simmer for 15 minutes.

Serves eight.

EGG DROP SOUP WITH SMOKED HAM

1 quart chicken broth
1 tablespoon cornstarch - approx.
1 well beaten egg
2 tablespoons minced green onions
4 tablespoons chopped smoked ham

Use a commercial seasoning base (available at restaurant supply companies) to make a richly flavored chicken broth. Bring the broth to a slow boil and very slowly add the beaten egg to the broth. Use a whisk to stir the egg, again slowly, in one direction, into the simmering broth.

Add the green onion and ham and cook for just a few minutes before serving. Mix the tablespoon cornstarch with

2 tablespoons cold water. Add to the soup and stir. Allow a few minutes for the broth to thicken.

Serves 5 - 6.

LOUISIANA CRAB GUMBO

3 quarts water
1 large onion, chopped
2 large stalks celery, chopped
1 can (28 ounces) whole tomatoes, crushed
Approx. 3 tablespoons beef base
¼ teaspoon black pepper
⅛ teaspoon red pepper
1 package (10 ounces) frozen mixed vegetables
1 tablespoon brown sugar
1 tablespoon Worcestershire sauce
2 tablespoons fresh parsley, minced
4 tablespoons butter
1 pound white crab meat
1 pound claw crab meat

Bring 3 quarts water to a boil in a large pot. Add 3 tablespoons beef base and stir. Taste to see that you have a flavorful beef broth. Add more base or more water as needed.

In a skillet sauté the celery and onions in melted butter until just tender. add them to the broth, butter and all. Add the minced parsley, black pepper, red pepper, brown sugar, Worcestershire sauce, and undrained crushed tomatoes. Bring all to a boil.

Add the frozen vegetables and the crab meat. Stir and bring to a simmer. Taste and adjust seasonings. Simmer at least 30 minutes.

MARYLAND CRAB SOUP

3 quarts beef broth
1 medium onion - chopped
2 large stalks celery - chopped
2 cans (1 pound each) crushed tomatoes
¼ teaspoon black pepper
¼ teaspoon red cayenne pepper
1 tablespoon fresh minced parsley
1½ to 2 packages (10 ounces) frozen mixed vegetables
1 pound claw crab meat
8 ounces regular or special crab meat
brown sugar to taste (about 1 tablespoon)
Worcestershire sauce to taste (about 2 teaspoons)
3 tablespoons butter

Melt 3 tablespoons butter in a large pot. Sauté the chopped celery and onion in the butter until cooked but not brown. Add the beef broth and crushed tomatoes and increase the heat to bring the soup to a simmer. Add the seasonings except for the brown sugar and Worcestershire sauce. Add the crab meat after picking out any shell pieces. Add the frozen mixed vegetables and return soup to a slow boil. Add brown sugar and Worcestershire sauce to taste. Allow the soup to simmer for 30 minutes and serve. Makes between 5 & 6 quarts of soup.

MONKFISH CHOWDER

3 tablespoons butter
1 pound monkfish fillets
3 tablespoons butter
¼ cup chopped onion
2 tablespoons chopped green pepper
2 tablespoons chopped celery
2 tablespoons chopped pimentos
1½ cups diced cooked potatoes
1 can (15 ounces) whole kernel corn
1 cup light cream
1 cup milk
dash each of salt & white pepper

Melt 3 tablespoons butter in a skillet over medium heat. Cut the monkfish fillets into thin strips and add them to the skillet. Cook and stir until cooked through - about 6 minutes.

Drain the fish on paper towels. Cut the strips of cooked fish across their length into bite size pieces.

In a sauce pan melt 3 tablespoons of butter. Add the onions, celery, and peppers. Cook until tender but not brown. Add the can of whole kernel corn (undrained), the cooked diced potatoes, and the pimentos. Add the cooked monkfish, 1 cup of light cream, 1 cup of milk, and salt and pepper. Stir to blend and heat to serving temperature. Avoid boiling.

Serves 4 - 5.

■ Use lids on pans to speed the cooking process. Liquids boil about 30% faster when a tight fitting lid is used.

SEAFOOD CHOWDER

4 tablespoons butter
½ cup chopped onion
½ cup chopped green pepper
2 cans (15 ounces each) whole kernel corn (undrained)
2 - 12 ounce packages logostinos (drained)
2 cups half & half
2 cups milk
salt & white pepper to taste

Melt butter in a large sauce pan. Add chopped peppers and onions and sauté until tender but not brown.

Add cans of undrained corn, logostinos, half & half, milk and salt & white pepper. Heat to near boiling point over medium heat. Do not allow to boil unless you can stir it constantly.

Serves 8 - 10. For smaller groups, divide all ingredient amounts in half. Works just as well in either quantity.

COCO-LOBSTER SOUP

12 ounces cooked lobster meat or logostinos
3 cups coconut milk (recipe follows)
1 teaspoon Kikkoman soy sauce
dash tabasco sauce
chopped parsley
2 tablespoons sherry wine (optional)
Coconut Milk

Pour 3 cups boiling whole milk over 3 cups dry grated coconut. Let stand twenty minutes. Strain the mixture, pressing with a spoon to separate as much milk as possible. Can be used in all recipes calling for coconut milk.

Combine lobster (or logostinos) with coconut milk, soy sauce, tabasco, and chopped parsley. Cook over low heat for about 20 minutes, but do not boil. If sherry is used, add it during the last 5 minutes of cooking. Garnish with a little more fresh parsley and serve immediately.

Serves four.

Salads

BACON & EGG SALAD

1 head of romaine lettuce
2 large stalks celery
¾ pound bacon cut raw in 1-inch pieces
5 hard boiled "mustard eggs"
("mustard eggs" are available in supermarket delis)
2 large tomatoes

Fry the precut bacon and drain on paper towels. Allow to cool. Refrigeration is optional.

Keep the head of romaine lettuce intact as you wash it under cold water. Wash the lettuce in an upright position. Turn it up side down and shake off the excess water.

Hold the lettuce around its girth and cut across the width. Start about 1 ½ inches from the butt and end about the same distance from the top. Use a serrated-edged knife. Put the romaine in a large bowl. Slice the celery on an angle and add to salad.

Add the cooked bacon to the salad. Slice or shop 3 of the 5 cooked eggs and add to the salad. Toss.

Slice the remaining two eggs with an egg slicer and layer on top of the greens. Cut the tomatoes into wedges and line the rim of the salad.

Serve with creamy Italian dressing or the dressing of your choice.

Serves 6 to 8.

■ The modern instant, or microwave, thermometers are great tools for helping us know when meats are done properly. Purchase one that registers 0 to 220 degrees. Insert the tip halfway through the meat and avoid touching bone. It will accurately tell you the internal temperature of the meat in just a few seconds. This style thermometer is never left in the meat while it cooks.

BELGIAN ENDIVE SALAD WITH BEETS

1 can (8¼ ounces) julienne beets
Green leaf or Boston lettuce
½ lb. Belgian endive
3 hard cooked egg

Line 4 salad plates with green leaf or Boston lettuce. Arrange endive leaves in a circular fashion, stems in the center, tips around the rim of each plate. Place one fourth of the julienne beets at the stem end of the endive. Drizzle with salad dressing and top with finely chopped par boiled eggs.

A good dressing to use is a vinaigrette with Dijon mustard. Simply whisk 1 tablespoon Dijon mustard into the Italian or vinaigrette bottled dressing of your choice.

■ Dry salad greens in a salad spinner, or with towels. Excess moisture will prevent salad dressings from adhering to the greens.

CABBAGE SLAW WITH LIME & HERB DRESSING

1 pound green cabbage -shredded
1 small red onion - minced
2 tablespoons minced fresh parsley
1 cucumber

Lime & Herb Dressing

⅓ cup lime juice
½ teaspoon garlic powder
¾ cup salad oil
dash each - salt & pepper
sugar to taste - a generous tablespoon for me

Whisk the dressing ingredients in a bowl and set aside. Whisk again just before dressing salad.

Skin the cucumber and cut it in half. Remove the seeds with a spoon or similar tool and cut the cucumber into crescent pieces.

Toss the shredded cabbage, minced onion, minced parsley, and cucumber together in a bowl. Whisk dressing and coat the salad.

I enjoy this salad best when it is refrigerated overnight. I use a gallon-size zip lock bag to seal in ingredients and aromas.

Serves 4.

CREAMY BACON COLE SLAW

1 medium head of cabbage (about 2 pounds)
4 - 6 strips bacon
1 bottle (16 ounces) Creamy Bacon Dressing
about 1 cup of milk

Cut the bacon strips into small pieces and cook until crisp. Drain on paper towels.

While the bacon cooks, discard the outer leaves of the cabbage that do not look up to par. Quarter the cabbage with a large knife. Cut away the exposed core from each section. Chop or shred the cabbage as fine or coarse as you like.

In a bowl pour out the bottled creamy bacon dressing. Pour some milk into the drained bottle. Seal and shake the bottle to fully drain. Add this mixture to the dressing in the bowl using a whisk to blend. You may add more milk to the dressing in the bowl if you want a thinner texture. This is a matter of personal preference.

Add the cooked bacon pieces to the dressing.

In another bowl add the dressing to the chopped cabbage in increments of about a cup. Toss the cabbage and dressing after each addition until you like the consistency. Save any remaining dressing to add to the slaw later, or for use on green salads.

Chill the slaw before serving.

Makes about 8 cups.

■ Wire whisks are indispensable when making sauces and gravies. The whisk is the best possible hand tool for the blending of ingredients and seasonings.

GREEN PEA SALAD

1 package (16 ounces) frozen peas
1 head iceberg lettuce
1 large stalk celery, chopped
1 large clove garlic, minced
2 cups French dressing

Thaw the peas under running water or overnight in the refrigerator. Drain them well.

Chop or tear the lettuce into bite sized pieces. Combine the peas with the minced garlic, the chopped celery, and the iceberg lettuce. Add the French dressing and toss gently but thoroughly. Allow the salad to set for about an hour in refrigeration. Stir occasionally.

Serves 8 to 10.

GREEN AND WAX BEAN SALAD WITH BACON

1 pound fresh green beans
¾ fresh wax beans
1 small red onion
10 slices of bacon
1 envelope Good Seasons Italian Dressing Mix
¼ cup vinegar
½ cup salad oil

Cut the raw bacon slices across their length at 1-inch intervals. Fry the bacon pieces, stirring often, and drain on paper towels when done.

While the bacon is frying, prepare the dressing mix using 2 tablespoons water, ¼ cup vinegar, and ½ cup salad oil. Shake the liquid ingredients in a sealed jar. Add package of dressing mix and shake again.

Cut or snap both beans into 1½-inch pieces. Bring a pot of water to boiling. Add beans and cook 8 to 10 minutes. Be sure to drain the beans while they are crisp tender.

Slice the red onion into quarter circles that are ⅛ inch thick.

Combine the beans, bacon, and red onion in a container with a tight-fitting lid. Pour about two thirds of the salad dressing over all and stir. Cover and refrigerate for about 45 minutes. Stir and taste the bean salad. Add more dressing if you feel it is needed.

Serves 12 - 15.

HAM & EGG SALAD WITH GARDEN TOMATOES

1 head romaine lettuce
5 hard-cooked eggs
3 slices smoked baked ham
2 large red ripe tomatoes

Dressing, Creamy Italian

1 cup sour cream
½ cup Miracle Whip
1 envelope Good Season's Italian Dressing Mix
½ cup light cream

To make the dressing, simply whisk the ingredients together in a large bowl. Transfer to a pourable container. Cover and refrigerate.

Wash and shake dry the head of romaine lettuce. Keep it intact. Cut across the length of the head in 1 inch slices. The lettuce will fall into bite sized pieces. Dry the cut lettuce with towels or in a salad spinner.

Cut the ham into bite-sized pieces and toss with the romaine.

Chop the hard-cooked eggs and spread them on the top of the salad. Cut the tomatoes into wedges and line them tip to tip around the outside edge of the salad howl. Place the tomato wedges skin side up to display their color. Pass the dressing to allow guests to pour their own.

■ Prepare your salad greens well in advance of your meal time. After drying your greens, cover them with a moist paper towel. They will stay crisp and fresh for hours in refrigeration.

GREEK SALAD WITH FETA CHEESE DRESSING

1 medium-sized head romaine lettuce
1 teaspoon fresh ground pepper
1 medium red onion - cut in strips
1 carrot - skinned and sliced
20 Greek olives
12 large fresh mushrooms - washed and sliced

Wash, dry, and cut romaine.

Peel and slice the carrot. Add to greens. Wash and slice mushrooms. Peel red onion and cut in half through the center of the root end. Lay onion halves on flat sides and cut in strips about ¼-inch wide. Use a small paring knife to peel Greek olives away from their pits. Each olive will yield 3 to 4 pieces. Add the carrots, mushrooms, red onion, and olive pieces to the greens. Refrigerate dry salad ingredients while you make Feta Dressing.

Feta Dressing

5 ounces Feta cheese
1 tablespoon dried chives
½ teaspoon garlic powder
2 tablespoons mayonnaise or salad dressing
1 tablespoon sour cream
1¼ cup light cream

Crumble the Feta cheese into a blender or food processor. Add the chives, garlic powder, mayonnaise, and sour cream. Blend the ingredients, using a pulsing action. Add the light cream as you continue to blend the dressing to a consistency of your liking.

Serve the salad in individual bowls and allow diners to dress their own.

Serves 6 to 8.

PASTA SALAD SUPREME

1 pound cooked pasta of choice
1 bottle (8 ounces) Robust Italian Dressing
4½ tablespoons Salad Supreme Seasoning
1 cucumber - chopped, bite size
2 ripe tomatoes - chopped, bite size

Cook pasta (spaghetti, small shells, macaroni, rotini, etc.) until just done. Drain and rinse with cold water.

Chop cucumber and tomatoes and toss with drained pasta.

Sprinkle 4½ tablespoons Salad Seasoning over pasta and vegetables and toss. Pour Italian dressing over all and mix gently but thoroughly. Cover. Chill 45 minutes before serving. Stir again before bringing to the table.

There are hundreds of variations to this and most other pasta salads. To try different ingredients separate about a 1½ cups of the base recipe salad. Add a few new ingredients and taste.

PICKLED CORN SALAD

½ cup chopped onions
½ cup diced green peppers
4 tablespoons chopped pimento
3 tablespoons sugar
¼ teaspoon salt
½ teaspoon celery salt
½ teaspoon dry mustard
½ cup cider vinegar
½ cup water
3 cups frozen whole kernel corn

Combine all ingredients except frozen corn. Bring to a boil in a saucepan. Lower heat, simmer for 10-12 minutes, covered. Stir occasionally.

After 10-12 minutes add the frozen corn. Cook until corn is just tender.

Serve pickled corn hot or cold.

When serving cold try serving it on lettuce leaves.

POLYNESIAN SHRIMP SALAD

8-10 cooked shrimp per guest served
⅓ cup chopped celery per serving
2 cups torn iceberg lettuce
2 teaspoons sesame seeds (toasted) per serving
1 teaspoon sesame oil per serving
¾ cup Miracle Whip (or mayonnaise) per serving
lemon and/or kiwi for garnish

Peel and devein the cooked shrimp. Put the shrimp in a bowl with the torn lettuce and chopped celery. Set aside.

In a dry skillet over medium heat, toast the sesame seeds. Shake the pan gently a few times to turn the sesame seeds.

When lightly browned set them aside to cool.

In another small bowl beat the sesame oil into the Miracle Whip while pouring the oil in a slow stream.

Transfer the sesame oil and Miracle Whip into the bowl with the shrimp, lettuce and celery and stir to coat those ingredients. Mix about half the toasted sesame seeds into the salad at this time.

Top the salad with the rest of the sesame seeds and serve with lemon and/or kiwi garnish.

■ To test to see if shrimp are cooked properly, pick out a large shrimp from the batch and taste it. If it is done, the whole batch is done. The time to taste test shrimp is when half or more of the shrimp have curled in half. Remove them from the heat, and drain them as soon as they are done. They will steam 3 or 4 more minutes in their shell as they cool.

POPPY SEED DRESSING

1⅓ cups sugar
2 teaspoons salt
2 teaspoons dry mustard
⅔ cup white vinegar
3 tablespoons each, finely chopped onion, poppy seeds
2 cups vegetable, or olive oil

Combine sugar, salt, dry mustard and vinegar. Add onion and mix well. Pour into blender and slowly add oil while blending on medium speed. Blend until thick. Stir in the poppy seeds. Store in the refrigerator for up to 4 weeks. If it separates, shake well or beat. Serve with fresh fruit salads.

QUICK CABBAGE SALAD

1 head napa cabbage
1 small head purple cabbage
2 carrots
1 bunch endive
cherry tomatoes

Slice napa across its length into bite-sized pieces. Slice and chop fine enough purple cabbage to add good color contrast to the napa. Shred the carrots coarsely and add to the salad.

Garnish the perimeter of the salad howl with endive leaves and cherry tomatoes.

Serve with your favorite cream-style dressing.

■ Whole, bone-in poultry yields 50 percent edible meat after cooking. A 6-pound roasting chicken will yield 3 pounds of cooked meat after a careful carving and picking of the cooked bird.

ROMAINE, MUSHROOM, OLIVE, & PEPPER SALAD

1 head romaine lettuce
10 large fresh mushrooms
15 extra large, pitted black olives
2 small red bell peppers

2 cups homemade buttermilk dressing (recipe follows)

Wash and dry the head of romaine lettuce, intact. Cut the lettuce in 1 inch strips across its length. Dry further in a towel if the greens are still wet. Place in a large bowl.

Wash, dry, and slice the mushrooms. Add them to the bowl. Slice the black olives in half lengthwise. Toss the olives with the greens and mushrooms.

Core and seed the red peppers, then rinse and dry them. Use a fork to roast them over an open flame. Cook them until they begin to soften, and their skins become only partially streaked with black burn marks from the flame. At least 70 percent of the pepper's skin should be bright red when the pepper begins to soften. This is a partial roasting. Cool the peppers, while mushrooms and black olives show their colors against the background of the greens. Serve with dressing of choice, or with homemade buttermilk dressing.

Buttermilk Dressing

1 cup Miracle Whip salad dressing
1 cup buttermilk
5-6 twists of fresh ground pepper
¼ teaspoon garlic powder
¼ teaspoon each crushed, dried basil leaves, oregano leaves

Shake the buttermilk container. Then whisk the ingredients in a bowl in no particular order. Makes 2 cups dressing.

ROMAINE & MUSHROOM SALAD

1 head romaine lettuce
12 ounces fresh mushrooms

Creamy Italian Dressing

8 ounces half & half light cream
4 tablespoons Miracle Whip
3 tablespoons sour cream
1 envelope Good Seasons Italian Dressing Mix

Wash romaine lettuce and discard any browned pieces. Slice the trimmed romaine across its length into bite-sized pieces.

Dry with towels or a salad spinner.

Wash and dry mushrooms and slice to a thickness of about ⅛ inch. Toss mushrooms and romaine in a salad bowl.

In a bowl whisk together the salad dressing ingredients.

If you feel you want another vegetable in this very simple salad, be sure to choose one that will offer a color contrast. Carrots cut in julienne strips would work well.

Serve the salad and allow guests to add dressing as they choose.

SALAD ON A STICK

Presenting salad vegetables on a skewer is an eye appealing way to serve a salad in a nonconventional manner. This presentation is more a method than a recipe. The ingredients will change with seasonal availability.

I suggest that you "cruise" your favorite produce department and select vegetables that offer good color contrasts. Cut or slice the vegetables into similar sizes, bite-size when possible.

Some vegetables, like carrots, may tend to split when pierced with a skewer. Allow these more brittle foods to come to room temperature before attempting to skewer them. Soaking them in heavily salted water also makes them more pliable.

Greens are best presented in the form of wedges, Iceberg lettuce lends itself well to wedge cutting.

When it is time to eat the salad hold the blunt end of the skewer between the tines of a fork with an inch of the skewer protruding. Use this end as a handle. Hold the fork steady and slowly pull out the skewer.

Serving suggestion: When using a non-oily dressing like ranch or thousand island, ladle a small pool of dressing on a salad plate. Then place the colorful salad kabob on the dressing.

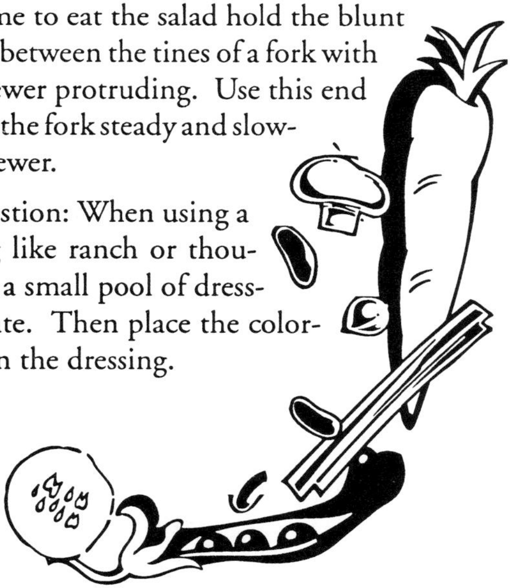

SPINACH SALAD

1 package (10 ounces) spinach
1 can (16 ounces) bean sprouts
8 to 10 slices bacon
5 hard-boiled eggs

Wash and dry the spinach. Tear it into small pieces, discarding the stems. Drain the bean sprouts and toss the spinach and bean sprouts in a large bowl.

Cut the bacon in small pieces while raw. Cook the bacon and drain on paper towels. Toss the cooled bacon with the spinach and sprouts.

Peel and dice the hard-boiled eggs and toss them with the other ingredients.

Spinach Salad Dressing

1 cup salad oil
¾ cup sugar
⅓ cup ketchup
¼ cup vinegar
1 tablespoon Worcestershire sauce
1 small onion, diced
dash salt

Mix all the ingredients except the sugar in a bowl or shaker. Add the sugar in 3 parts, stirring or shaking after each addition.

Allow the diner to dress his or her salad, rather than dressing the whole bowl of ingredients.

SPINACH SALAD WITH BACON & SHRIMP

1 package (10 ounces) fresh leaf spinach
1 can (16 ounces) bean sprouts (or 2½ cups fresh-blanched)
10 slices bacon - cut and fried
4 large eggs - hard-cooked
1 pound salad shrimp or larger size cut bite-sized

Carefully wash the spinach to remove any sand or grit. Tear the spinach leaves into bite size pieces and discard the stems. Dry the torn greens and put them in a large bowl. Toss the bean sprouts, shrimp, and the cooked bacon with the spinach. Dice the hard-cooked eggs and sprinkle over the top of the salad.

Pass the salad undressed and allow each diner to treat his or her salad with spinach salad dressing on page 68.

TACO SALAD

1 pound ground chuck
1 head iceberg lettuce
3 cups enchilada sauce
12 ounces cojack cheese - shredded
1 bag (14½ ounces) of Doritos
4 medium tomatoes - chopped
1 large red onion - chopped
½ teaspoon garlic powder
½ teaspoon each cumin, chili powder

Place the ground chuck in a sauté pan over medium heat. Separate the ground beef with wooden utensils. Season the ground chuck with ½ teaspoon each of garlic powder, cumin, and chili powder. Sauté the seasoned meat until just done. Remove the pan from the burner and spoon off any excess fat. Taste and adjust seasonings. (the seasoned meat may be served hot or cold).

Tear the lettuce into bite-sized pieces.

To construct each salad — line the bottom of the salad bowl with a few crumbled doritos. Next put in a small amount of chopped lettuce. Add about ½ cup of the cooked ground chuck. Add a few tablespoons of chopped onions. Add more lettuce. Now sprinkle another ½ cup meat over the lettuce. Spread ¾ cup chopper tomatoes over the meat and lettuce. Add a few more red onions. Top the salad with a generous amount of shredded cojack cheese. Arrange Doritos around the rim of the salad bowl with points facing outward to give a starburst effect. Pour about ½ cup enchilada sauce over salad and serve. (Enchilada sauce may be not or cold.)

Serve extra enchilada sauce on the side in a small cup.

Makes up to 8 salads.

RUBBERMAID HOME SALAD BAR

Salads are popular and good for you, but they're a pain in the neck to make. Consequently, we don't eat as many salads as we should. In an effort to solve this problem I purchased a compartmentalized Rubbermaid container with a tight-sealing lid. On the weekend I slice or chop celery, carrots, cucumbers, purple cabbage, and mushrooms and load the portable "salad bar."

With everything pre-cut anyone can make a salad in minutes. One simply chops some lettuce and adds to it from the salad bar.

When we all sit down to eat together I give everyone a plate of chopped lettuce. The salad bar is placed in the middle of the table and everyone builds his or her own salad.

It's easy to substitute other salad bar items to offer variety. Examples are black olives, shredded cheese, croutons, Pepperidge Farms gold fish, bacon bits, tomatoes, green peppers, feta cheese, alfalfa sprouts, or napa cabbage.

CREAMED LETTUCE

A popular salad during my active career as a chef was creamed lettuce. The kitchen staffs loved it because it was so easy to make and serve.

Simply place a wedge of iceberg lettuce on a salad plate and drizzle it with cole slaw dressing. That's it. It tastes great.

To convert creamed lettuce to Dutch Lettuce, simply chop the lettuce and add pieces of cooked bacon and chopped hard-boiled eggs.

STEMMED SALAD GREENS

Long-stemmed salad greens such as napa cabbage and romaine lettuce lend themselves to quick salad-making because they slice into bite-sized pieces so easily. Simply slice them across their length in one inch increments. Return the uncut portion to the crisper. Trim off a half-inch from the cut end before using for the next salad.

Entrées

SUGGESTIONS WHEN BUYING STEAKS

1. Select steaks that are fine-grained, well-marbled with fat, and which have good color.

2. When broiling, grilling, or frying, select steaks which are cut from the short loin or the rib:

   Loin or Strip Steak

   Tenderloin or Fillet

   Porterhouse

   T-Bone

   Rib Steak

   Rib Eye or Delmonico

3. Two money-saving exceptions to #2 come from the chuck. They are the chuck Delmonico and the Spencer Steak. You can broil, fry, or grill either of these steaks. However, I recommend that you don't cook them past the medium point of doneness.

4. When possible, buy U.S.D.A. CHOICE beef steaks. Your chances for tender juicy results improve dramatically when you buy CHOICE steaks.

5. If you are buying steaks that are bone-in, select the steaks using suggestion #1 as a guide but also look for white bones. Dark bones indicate older animals.

6. For guests or family members with average appetites, purchase 10-12 ounces of bone-in meat or 6-8 ounces of boneless meat per person.

BARBECUE PRIMER

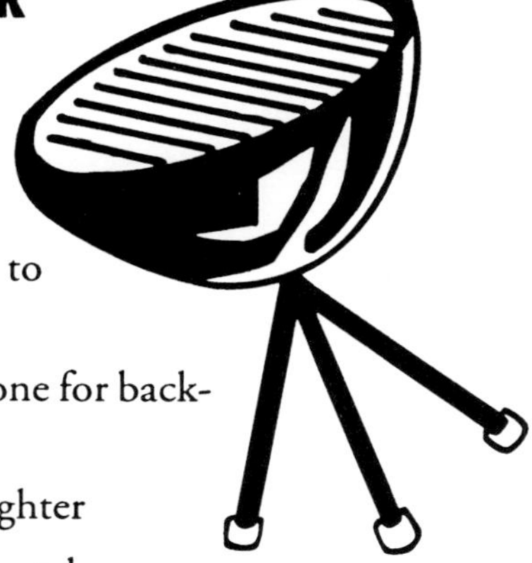

Here are some hints and suggestions for the barbecue season:

■ On your first trip to the store purchase

Two bags of charcoal - one for backup

Two cans of charcoal lighter

Two boxes of kitchen matches

Two boxes of wide heavy duty aluminum foil

When you empty the first package of any of the above supply, it is time to purchase it again. This way you will always have a working supply and a back-up supply.

■ Gas grill users can purchase new or rebuilt propane tanks and use them for back-ups.

■ Never light a gas grill without opening the lid before turning on the gas supply. Also, the lid must remain up while lighting the grill. You can close the lid once the grill is lit to speed warm-up time.

■ You will become a much more confident barbecue cook if you develop consistency in your methods.

Use the same grid height for the same foods.

Use the same amount of charcoal or gas setting.

Start with the same temperature food each time.

Refrigerated steaks require longer cooking times than steaks that have reached room temperature. Select one way or the other and stay with that method.

■ Select steaks of the same thickness.

■ Select a method for testing doneness and use it consistently.

Professionals test steaks by touching them with their finger. You can acquire an accurate "touch' for doneness but it requires cooking a lot of steaks on a weekly basis. If you develop consistent procedures, I believe your best gauge for accuracy is your watch: Four minutes per side for rare. Five minutes per side for medium, etc.

■ Line the firebox of your charcoal grill (each time) with heavy duty aluminum foil for good heat reflection, less wear and tear on your grill, and for easy clean-up.

■ Select an area outside that is level, free from fire hazards, away from areas where the kids play, and out from under trees and large bushes.

■ Select an area that is least affected by high winds. Wind and strong breezes inhibit lighting and slow cooking times.

■ After a warm-up period (10-12 minutes for gas grills and 30 minutes for charcoal) hold your hand about 2 inches from the cooking grid. Count "one-thousand one, one thousand two". At this point you should have to pull your hand back from the heat. If so, your heat is right for grilling steaks.

■ Brush a little vegetable oil on new or clean grill racks once while heating and again when hot to inhibit sticking.

■ Assemble your ingredients and tools and have them at hand before you begin cooking.

■ Use metal tongs for handling foods around the grill or broiler. Almost all foods are moist whether raw or in the cooking process. Tongs provide secure handling and do not puncture foods, thus releasing valued juices. Don't use forks for this purpose.

■ A heated metal serving platter is very handy for bringing food from the grill to the table. It's appetizing to bring the steaks to the table "sizzling" on a hot platter.

■ Keep a fire extinguisher near your barbecue area.

■ Learn your heated grill surface. You may have hot spots and cool spots of which you will want to be aware.

■ Don't overload your functional grill surface. Overloading your cooking surface makes a hectic cooking experience instead of a pleasant one.

■ Avoid putting cooked food on a plate which you used to carry raw food to the grill. Put raw food on waxed paper and then on a plate to transport it to the grill area. Discard the waxed paper once the food is put on the grill.

■ Precook bone-in chicken, or beef or pork ribs, before finishing them on the outdoor grill. Baste either meat, generously, with the same sauce you'll use on the grill. Place the meat in a greased baking pan. Cook, covered with a loose foil tent, in a preheated 350 degree oven for 25 minutes per pound for chicken, and 45 minutes per pound for pork. Finish the meat on the grill for 10 to 15 minutes, or until the meat is nicely browned.

■ Do not use a marinade, which was used with raw meat, as a basting sauce on the grill unless you boil it for about 5 minutes.

■ Place steaks on a hot grill on a 45 degree angle. Cook a few minutes and turn the steaks to a 45 degree angle (same side up and same side down) in the opposite direction. Repeat when doing the other side. This "marks" your steak with attractive diamond shapes.

HEINZ 57 & HONEY BARBECUE SAUCE

Not very complicated, but oh so very good! Simply mix 2 parts Heinz 57 sauce with 1 part honey. That's it. Brush this sauce on pre-cooked pork or beef ribs, or chicken, as you finish them on the grill. Baste both sides frequently. This sauce is a little expensive, but it is an absolute winner.

EASTERN SHORE STYLE BARBECUE SAUCE

¾ cup melted butter or margarine
⅓ cup white vinegar
1 teaspoon poultry seasoning
1 teaspoon salt
1 teaspoon pepper
2 teaspoons brown sugar
2 teaspoons Old Bay Seasoning

This sauce will burn if not watched closely. Simply turn and baste the meats frequently to keep in control. You'll get some flare ups. Just keep the meats rotating. It's worth a little extra work!

OLD BAY BARBECUE SAUCE

1½ cups ketchup
½ cup brown sugar
1½ tablespoons Old Bay Seasoning

Mix together, heat and serve over meat or poultry.

CHINESE BARBECUE SAUCE

3 cloves garlic
1 teaspoon salt
1 tablespoon light soy sauce
1 tablespoon honey
1 tablespoon dry sherry
½ teaspoon five spice powder

Crush the garlic and salt together. Combine with other ingredients in a large bowl. Marinate up to 1 pound lean pork or chicken, cut into strips. Mix well so meat is well coated. Marinate meat for at least 15 minutes.

BARBECUED BEEF SHORT RIBS

4 pounds beef short ribs
¾ cup flour
1 teaspoon salt
1 teaspoon pepper
2 tablespoons brown sugar
1 tablespoon cider vinegar
½ teaspoon dry mustard
¾ cup bottled chili sauce
¾ cup beer
1 cup beef broth
2 teaspoons McCormick's dry barbecue spice

Combine flour with the salt and pepper. Coat the ribs all over with the seasoned flour. Brown the ribs in oil in a skillet, turning several times.

Mix the brown sugar, vinegar, dry mustard, ketchup, beer, and beef broth in a bowl. Place the browned ribs in a casserole or shallow baking dish. Cover the meat with the sauce mixture. Bake at 350 degrees for 1½ hours or until tender. Check while cooking for excessive browning. Cover with a loose foil tent if the meat is becoming too dark.

Try this dish in your 6-quart pressure cooker. Brown the meat as directed. Then place the meat and sauce mixture in your pressure cooker. Seal the lid and fit the control valve in place.

Heat the cooker over high heat until the control valve jiggles steadily, about 8-10 minutes. Back the heat down to where the control valve jiggles sporadically, 3 to 5 times per minute, and cook for 25 minutes. Relieve the pressure by allowing the cooker to cool, off the heat, for 5 minutes. Then run cold water over the lid of the cooker for 3 minutes. Lift off the valve and open the lid.

Just before serving the short ribs, after either cooking method, sprinkle with McCormick's dry barbecue seasoning.

BARBECUED PRIME RIB BONES

The 6- to 8-inch long beef spare ribs you see in the butcher's case are the ribs that surround the rib roast. The rib roast, when oven-roasted, becomes prime rib. These meaty ribs come from a good neighborhood on the carcass. They are not expensive and the meat is tender and juicy.

I recommend cutting the ribs into single bone portions before cooking. This exposes more surface area for seasonings to penetrate.

2 pounds beef spare ribs per adult portion
2 cups water
beef base (or dry bouillon mix)
1 bottle (10 ounces) Heinz 57 Sauce
McCormick's Montreal Steak Seasoning

Cut ribs into single bone portions.

Heat the water in a sauce pan. Add 3 teaspoons beef base and stir. Pour the beef broth in a roasting pan. Place a rack in the pan and put the beef ribs in the pan with the curved underside of the bones facing down. Roast over the broth at 350 degrees for 40 minutes.

Pour the Heinz 57 sauce in a bowl and dilute it with ⅓ cup of the broth from the roasting pan. Stir to blend. Sprinkle the ribs lightly with Montreal steak seasoning and brush them on all sides with the diluted Heinz 57 sauce.

Cook the ribs on a hot grill for 8 to 10 minutes. Baste again with the steak sauce as they cook.

BARBECUE STEAKS

For a change in your steak diet, who not try an old fashioned method for seasoning steaks for grilling or broiling? Simply marinate your favorite cut of loin or rib steak in the barbecue sauce of your choice.

To marinate a 1-inch thick beef steak of any variety it will take about 45 minutes at room temperature or about 3 hours under refrigeration. The colder the temperature, the slower the marinating process.

When you are ready to cook simply remove the steaks from the marinade and allow the excess sauce to drain off before grilling or barbecuing. The cooking process remains the same except for the cooking temperature. I recommend that you use medium heat because the molasses and tomato products used in most barbecue sauces tend to burn over high heat.

I have been concocting barbecue sauces for 15 years but still find it hard to improve on the commercial sauces available on the grocery shelf when marinating beef steaks. My personal preference is for the commercial sauces that feature a smoked flavor.

PEPPERY BARBECUED BEEF

4 N.Y. Strip, or chuck Delmonico steaks (8 ounces each)
2 tablespoons crushed black peppercorns
½ cup cooking oil
¼ cup hoison sauce
2 tablespoons Kikkoman soy sauce
2 cloves garlic, minced

Slash the fat at the side of each steak, being careful not to cut into the meat. Press the crushed peppercorns into both sides of each steak using the palm of your hand.

Combine the cooking oil, soy sauce, hoison sauce, and garlic in a gallon size zip lock bag. Place the steaks in the bag and marinate 1 hour at room temperature or 6 hours in refrigerator. Turn the bag over occasionally. Be gentle so a minimum of pepper is dislodged.

Drain the steaks and reserve marinade. Cook the marinade at a simmer for about 5 minutes. Add a little water if it loses volume.

Grill the steaks, basting occasionally with the marinade, to desired degree of doneness.

For an Oriental presentation slice the steaks across the grain in thin strips and layer on a platter next to rice or vegetables.

CHUCK DELMONICO or CHUCK EYE STEAK

I would like to share with beef steak fans a "butcher's secret." The secret is a great steak that is not well known. Meat shops label it as chuck eye steak, chuck fillet, or chuck Delmonico. For our discussion we will call it chuck Delmonico.

This steak is cut from a small roast that comes from the chuck, which is the beef's front shoulder. Because the front shoulder is a working muscle, most meat from that section requires long cooking times with low heat and lots of moisture (braising). The little roast that supplies the chuck Delmonico is an exception. I can only guess that it is positioned in such a way that it is protected from the bulk of the work done by the shoulder.

The chuck Delmonico steak is smallish in size, most average about 6 to 8 ounces. It is more tender than a New York strip and is usually about a $1.50 per pound less expensive. You can grill, fry, of broil this steak with wonderful results. It will be tender and juicy.

The catch is that in an entire 1,200 pound beef there are only two roasts (which yield the chuck Delmonico) weighing about 1½ to 2 pounds each. This means that meat shops have never aggressively marketed this roast or the steaks because that would create a demand that could not be filled. Since some meat shops don't display this cut in either form, you must ask for it in advance. Call the meat department very early in the morning or a day in advance. A spontaneous order might mean that the butcher must break down a 70-pound chuck to get you a few 8-ounce steaks.

The little roast, called a chuck Delmonico roast, or chuck eye roast, can be roasted like a rib roast to make a mock prime rib. When you buy this meat in roast form you can also cut your own steaks and save a few cents per pound on purchase price.

I hope you will try this great cut of beef. Remember that if your store does not already display it, you should give that butcher some notice. Talk with him in person to make sure he understands which cut you mean. Terminology is different in every shop. Make sure he knows that this is a small roast from the chuck that, when cut into steaks, can be cooked quickly using dry heat methods such as grilling, broiling, and frying. Then he'll know what you mean. He's been taking them home for years.

OLD FASHIONED PAN FRIED STEAK

Here's a quick and easy way to prepare loin or rib steaks. For those on salt restricted diets it will be obvious that the kosher salt must be eliminated.

4 beef steaks cut from the short loin or rib
3 tablespoons melted beef fat
(vegetable oil can be substituted)
1½ tablespoons coarse or kosher salt
⅓ cup water or mild beef broth

Heat a large, heavy, skillet over medium heat. Melt beef fat trimmings (from the steaks) to yield 3 tablespoons of liquid fat. Or after the skillet is medium hot add 3 tablespoons vegetable oil. When your fat or oil is hot sprinkle the course salt in the skillet. Distribute it evenly in the skillet with a wooden spatula. Turn the heat to high and add the steaks to the pan. Seer both sides of the steaks for about 2 minutes or until they reach a dark brown color.

Remove the skillet from the heat. Turn the heat back to medium. After skillet rests off the heat for 1 or 2 minutes, and before you return it to the burner, add the ⅓ cup water or broth to the skillet. Scrape the skillet bottom with a spatula to deglaze the skillet. You shouldn't have to remove the steaks from the skillet. Just go slowly and gently. Cover the skillet and return it to the heat. Cook covered over medium heat for about 5 minutes to finish the steaks to medium rare to medium. This applies to 1-inch thick steaks. Do not use the pan broth when serving the steaks. It will be very salty.

TERIYAKI STEAK

1 bottle (10 ounces) Kikkoman soy sauce
4 steaks (8 to 10 ounces each) from the loin
2 plastic zip-lock style food storage bags

Trim the steaks of any excess fat. Pour ½ the Kikkoman in each plastic bag. Put 2 steaks in each bag and seal each bag so that it doesn't leak. Marinate the steaks at room temperature for about 45 minutes (or 3 hours or more under refrigeration). Turn the steaks about every 30 minutes.

Grill or broil the steaks as you would any raw strip steak to the desired degree of doneness.

Baste the steaks with the Kikkoman marinade as they cook.

■ Use wooden utensils. Wood will not scrape or scratch your cookware when stirring or handling food. If a wood utensil is inadvertently left over heat, it will not burn your hand as seriously as a metal or plastic tool in the same circumstance.

STEAK AU POIVRE

4 teaspoons whole black peppercorns
4 beef loin steaks - 1 inch thick
4 tablespoons butter or margarine
¼ cup chopped shallots or green onions
½ cup water
2 teaspoons powdered au jus mix
3 tablespoons brandy

Coarsely crack the peppercorns with mortar and pestle or with spoon in a metal mixing bowl. Grinding the peppercorns with a peppermill set on a course setting works fine. Slash the fat edge of your steaks at 1-inch intervals being careful to only cut the fat and not the meat. Sprinkle ½ teaspoon of cracked peppercorns over each steak. Rub firmly into the surface of each steak. Turn the steaks and repeat the process on the other side.

In a large skillet melt 2 tablespoons butter. Cook the steaks over medium-high heat to desired doneness, turning as needed. Allow about 5 minutes per side for medium - medium rare doneness.

Transfer steaks to a hot platter and keep hot.

Melt 2 more tablespoons butter in the same skillet and cook shallots until tender but not brown. Add water and au jus mix; boil rapidly for about 1 minute. Scrape bottom of skillet while mixture boils. Stir in the brandy and cook 1 minute more. Pour over steaks and serve.

Serves 4.

■ When placing foods in hot oils or liquids, use tongs and lay the food in the pan in a direction away from you. Hot splashes will hit your stove top, not your wrist and arm.

ROAST PRIME RIB OF BEEF

1 beef rib roast (4 pounds)
Kitchen Bouquet or Gravy Master browning sauces
5 tablespoons dry (powdered) au jus mix

Select a roasting pan large enough to accommodate the beef roast. Place a wire rack in the roasting pan to keep the meat above the pan juices.

Boil about 3½ cups water and add 2½ tablespoons dry au jus mix. Stir and taste. Adjust seasoning to taste. Pour about 1½ cups liquid au jus into roasting pan.

Place the roast fat side up on the rack in the roasting pan. Using a plastic sandwich bag as a mit over one hand, rub a few tablespoons browning sauce over the entire surface of the meat. Pat the remaining dry au jus mix onto the top and sides of the meat.

Place the pan with the prepared meat in the center of a preheated 325 degree oven. Roast the meat until the internal temperature reaches 135° F. for rare, or 145° F. for medium. Check with an instant reading thermometer at the two-hour point. Baste the meat occasionally while roasting. Add a little water if you need more liquid in the roasting pan.

Combine the pan juices with the remaining boiled au jus to serve at the table.

Allow the meat to rest at room temperature (15 to 20 minutes) before slicing and serving.

■ To save about $1.50 per pound with no loss in quality, use the little roast from which chuck Delmonico steaks are cut instead of the rib roast. You may need two or more to equal the size of a small or medium rib roast, but your savings will remain the same per pound. I know of no proper name for the marvelous little cut of meat that has been the butcher's secret for years. You'll have to call the meat manager before you visit the store to give him time to cut them for you. Describe the roast(s) to him just as I have above. Please don't tell him how you discovered his secret.

INDIVIDUAL BEEF WELLINGTON

I will give you the recipe for one serving of Beef Wellington. You can multiply it by the number of guests you plan to serve. Allow yourself plenty of prep time. The recipe is by no means difficult, but it does take time.

1 beef fillet steak (5 ounces)
Kitchen Bouquet
1 puff pastry square (5 inches by 5 inches)
1 beaten egg
⅓ pound ground veal
garlic powder
minced fresh parsley
Worcestershire Sauce
3 large mushrooms
1 tablespoon minced onion
salt & pepper
butter
flour
2 cups rich beef stock or au jus

Prepare a pâté by sautéing the ground veal with about a tablespoon of melted butter. Season the veal while it is sautéing with the mushrooms (minced), the parsley, garlic powder, Worcestershire Sauce, minced onions, salt & pepper and any other spice you choose. When the veal and accessories are done blend them in a food processor or blender to a consistency that will spread. The pâté mixture should not be too fine. A few small lumps will not detract from the dish. Set aside at room temperature.

Set your oven at 450 degrees. Grease a muffin/cupcake pan. Put a teaspoon of butter and a teaspoon of water in the greased muffin slot. Smear the steak with Kitchen Bouquet all over. Place the steak, with the grain of the meat running vertically, in a greased muffin slot or indentation. Place the steak and pan in the oven. The steak must be watched closely for doneness at this high heat. The best way to determine doneness is to probe it with an instant reading thermometer. When it reaches 110 degrees in the center of the steak, take it out of the oven. You have already browned the steak with Kitchen Bouquet so it could become charred. If the steaks begins to darken excessively, cover it loosely with foil.

Prepare a rich beef gravy using the flour and butter to make a roux. Cook the roux (equal amounts of butter and flour - melt the butter and stir in the flour and stir as it cooks) for about five minutes. Stir in the beef broth or au jus. Raise the heat to medium-high and stir until thick and bubbly. The portions for a gravy to amply serve two servings of Beef Wellington are - 4 tablespoons butter, 4 tablespoons flour, and 2 cups broth. A dark gravy enhances the plate presentation of this dish. Add drops of Kitchen Bouquet and stir until you are happy with the color. Keep your gravy hot while you assemble and finish the Wellington.

Lay a sheet of thawed puff pastry on your counter. Spread the puff pastry with the pâté mixture to a thickness of between ¼ and ½ inch. Place the steak on the pâté and pastry, again with the grain running vertically. Carefully wrap the steak, folding the corners up and over the fillet. Turn it over and place it on a greased baking sheet. Smear it all over with the beaten egg mixed with 1 tablespoon water.

Bake the Wellington at 400 degrees for about 15 minutes or until the puff pastry is nicely browned. When ready to serve, stir your gravy and pour a pool of it on your serving plate. Then place the Wellington in the center of the pool of brown gravy. Garnish with a colorful piece of fruit or vegetable and a sprig of parsley or watercress.

BEEF BURGUNDY

6 tablespoons butter
6 tablespoons flour
6 cups richly flavored beef broth
3 tablespoons bacon drippings
loin steaks or roast (1¾ pound) cubed bite size
4 additional tablespoons butter
3 cups chopped fresh mushrooms
1 cup chopped onions
¾ teaspoon garlic powder
1 teaspoon dried basil
1 tablespoon fresh minced parsley
1 tablespoon tomato paste
salt & pepper to taste
Burgundy wine to taste

Prepare a rich gravy by melting 6 tablespoons butter in a large sauce pan. Stir in 6 tablespoons of flour. Stir and cook over medium heat for about 5 minutes. Remove the pan from the heat and add 6 cups of rich beef broth that has been allowed to reach room temperature. Raise the heat to medium high. Stir with a whisk and cook until the gravy bubbles and thickens. Set the gravy over low heat.

In a large skillet containing 3 tablespoons bacon drippings fry 1¾ pounds beef, cubed bite-size. Beef steaks and roasts from the loin produce the most tender results. Cook the cubed beef until nicely browned. Add the browned beef to the gravy.

In the beef skillet melt 4 tablespoons butter and cook 3 cups chopped fresh mushrooms and 1 cup chopped onion until lightly browned. Add the cooked mushrooms and onions to the gravy.

While bringing the gravy to a simmer, season it with ½ teaspoon garlic powder, 1 teaspoon dried basil, 1 tablespoon fresh minced parsley, 1 tablespoon tomato paste, and salt and pepper to taste. Simmer the recipe for about 30 minutes.

Then add Burgundy wine to taste. Begin with ¼ cup. Stir. Allow to cook for a few minutes and then taste the gravy. The taste of the Burgundy wine should be evident, but not overpowering. If the taste of the wine is too subtle, add a few more tablespoons. Taste again. Repeat as necessary until you are pleased with the flavor. Simmer the stew for another 30 minutes. Taste and adjust seasonings before serving. Serve over hot buttered noodles.

Serves 4 - 5.

MEATBALL STROGANOFF

3½ cups beef gravy
2 tablespoons tomato paste
⅓ cup sour cream
1 can (15 ounces) mushroom stems & pieces
2 tablespoons fresh minced parsley
1 cup chopped onions
2 tablespoons butter
24 bite-sized cooked meatballs
8 ounces egg noodles

While warming the beef gravy over medium heat, sauté the chopped onion in 2 tablespoons melted butter until cooked but not browned.

Raise the heat under the gravy to bring it to a simmer. Add the tomato paste and stir with a whisk to blend. Add the sour cream and whisk again. Next add the onions, mushrooms, and parsley. Stir with a spoon to mix. Finally, add the cooked meatballs and cook for about 10 minutes while the noodles are cooking.

Cook the egg noodles (starting with 8 ounces uncooked) until just done. Drain well but don't rinse. Place the noodles in a large serving bowl. Pour the meatballs and stroganoff gravy over the noodles.

Serves 4.

PARMESAN MEATBALLS

1 pound ground chuck
⅓ cup grated parmesan cheese
2 tablespoons fresh minced parsley
¼ cup minced fresh onion
½ cup dried bread crumbs
½ teaspoon garlic powder
½ teaspoon dried basil
¼ teaspoon oregano
¼ teaspoon pepper
¼ teaspoon salt
1 large beaten egg
water to moisten
2 cups seasoned tomato sauce

Mix the first 11 ingredients together in a bowl. Add water, a little at a time, if needed, to moisten the mixture. Moisten your hands and form the meat mixture into meatballs.

Brown the meatballs in butter over medium heat in a wide skillet. Turn them often as they cook. Rotate the meatballs from pan center to pan edge as they brown.

When all the meatballs are browned, carefully pour off the excess fat. Turn the heat to medium-high. Add the seasoned tomato sauce to the skillet and return the pan to the heat. If you do not have a seasoned tomato sauce on hand, add a pinch or two of garlic powder, basil, parsley, oregano, and salt and pepper to a few cups of canned tomato sauce. The meatballs are ready to serve after they simmer 15 minutes in the sauce. Turn them a few times while they cook in the sauce.

Recipe makes 15 - 20 meatballs.

VEAL SCALLOPINI

4 veal cutlets (4 ounces each)
flour for dredging
6 tablespoons butter
¼ cup sherry
2 tablespoons minced fresh parsley
12 ounces fresh mushrooms - sliced
salt & pepper

Pound veal cutlets with a mallet to tenderize. Pound the veal firmly enough to flatten but not so hard as to tear the meat. Dredge the veal cutlets in flour. Sauté in melted butter in a large skillet for 3-4 minutes per side. Season with salt and pepper and add sherry wine. Add parsley and mushrooms. Sauté for 10 minutes more.

Serves 2.

■ Store herbs and spices out of direct sunlight, and away from the heat. Never keep them above your stove. There's a chance you'll drop them in a hot pan and get splashed, and burned, with a hot cooking liquid.

VEAL STEAKS WITH CRAB & MUSHROOMS

2 boneless veal steaks (6 to 8 ounces each)
2 cups thinly sliced fresh mushrooms
6 tablespoons butter
2 tablespoons water or beef broth
⅓ pound lump crab meat
salt & pepper to taste

Pound veal steaks lightly with a mallet and season with salt & pepper. Melt 2 tablespoons butter in a skillet and sauté the veal steaks on both sides until done. Cooking time will depend on the thickness of the veal steaks. About 4 minutes per side over medium high heat will handle the average veal steak. Remove the veal steaks to a warm platter.

Add 2 tablespoons water or beef broth to the hot skillet and deglaze the pan. Pour the resulting pan sauce over the cooked veal steaks.

Sauté the crab meat in 2 tablespoons butter and pour over the veal steaks.

You may want to bring a second large skillet into play and sauté the mushrooms and crab meat together and at the same time. Keep the mushrooms and the crab meat separated in the pan so that they can be layered on the steaks appropriately before serving.

Serves 2.

WIENER SCHNITZEL WITH HAZELNUT BUTTER

¼ pound butter
4 thin veal steaks
salt & pepper
flour for dredging
2 large eggs, beaten with 1 tablespoon water
4 tablespoons vegetable oil
2 tablespoons butter
seasoned bread crumbs for coating the veal

Melt the ¼ pound butter in a skillet over medium heat. Continue cooking until the butter becomes light brown in color. Do not allow the butter to get very brown or it will become bitter. The lightly browned butter takes on a pleasant nutty flavor. Thus the name hazelnut butter.

Pound the veal steaks with a mallet to tenderize. Season with salt & pepper and dredge in flour.

Dip the floured veal steaks in the egg wash and coat them with the seasoned bread crumbs. Gently press the steaks to help the bread crumbs to adhere.

Heat the oil and 2 tablespoons butter in a skillet over medium high heat. Sauté the veal steaks for about 4 minutes per side until nicely browned. Serve the veal with hazelnut butter poured over them.

Serves 2 to 4 depending on the size of the veal steaks.

CAJUN CHICKEN

2 skinned boneless chicken breast halves
per guest served

½ teaspoon onion powder
½ teaspoon garlic powder
½ teaspoon ground white pepper
½ teaspoon ground red pepper
½ teaspoon ground black pepper
½ teaspoon dried thyme
¼ teaspoon salt
3 tablespoons melted butter

In a small bowl combine the dry spices. Stir.

Pound the breast fillets with a mallet to tenderize and to even the thickness of the fillets.

Heat a large iron (or thick aluminum) skillet over high heat. The skillet should be dry. While the skillet is heating, brush the breast fillets with the melted butter. Coat one side with the dry seasoning mixture.

Add the breast fillets to the skillet, seasoned side down. Drizzle the remaining butter over the exposed, unseasoned side of each fillet. Now season this side of the fillets with the cajun seasoning. Cook uncovered over high heat about 3-4 minutes on each side, or until blackened. The fillets are done when the juices are clear. Cut one piece near the center to check doneness if you are in doubt.

CITY CHICKEN

2 pounds boneless chicken
8 bamboo skewers (6 inches long)
flour, salt & pepper
poultry seasoning
1 can each - beef and chicken broth
celery leaves
bulb garlic, sliced
sliced onion
parsley
3 tablespoons vegetable oil

Cut the boneless chicken into approximately one inch cubes. Use all white meat, all dark meat, or a combination of both, according to the preference of your guests. Lay the cubed chicken on waxed paper after washing. Sprinkle with salt, pepper, and poultry seasoning.

Skewer the seasoned chicken cubes on the bamboo skewers. The chicken pieces should be touching, but don't press them too tightly. Use 5 pieces per skewer.

Dredge the skewered chicken on all sides with flour.

Brown the skewered chicken in oil on all sides. When brown, place the kabobs in a shallow baking pan with 1 can chicken broth and 1 can beef broth. Add garlic, onion, celery leaves, and fresh parsley to the broth for seasoning. Cover tightly with aluminum foil and bake at 350 for at least one hour. Turn the kabobs once during baking time.

■ Aluminum foil has a shiny side and a dull side. When wrapping food or covering dishes to be baked, put the dull side facing out. The dull side absorbs more heat and will aid in cooking. When lining flat cooking sheets for broiling, place the shiny side up. It will reflect heat to the food.

EASTERN SHORE BARBECUE CHICKEN

6 chicken drumsticks
6 chicken thighs
1 cup vegetable oil
⅓ cup white vinegar
1 teaspoon poultry seasoning
1 teaspoon salt
1 teaspoon pepper
2 teaspoons brown sugar
2 teaspoons Old Bay Seasoning

Mix the last 7 ingredients in a bowl. Stir vigorously with a whisk just before transferring the sauce to a large shallow baking dish.

Place the chicken parts in the baking dish. Turn each piece to coat with the sauce.

Bake the chicken, uncovered, in a 350 degree oven for 25 minutes. Turn the chicken pieces and cook 25 minutes longer. Check the pan for moisture during each 25 minute cooking period. Add water if the pan is too dry. Natural juices from the chicken should moisten the pan, but check.

The chicken can now be rested for a later serving or taken right to the grill. In either case finish the chicken over a hot grill to impart outdoor flavor, coloring, and grill marks.

You may also want to marinate the chicken in the sauce before cooking. Just place it in gallon size zip lock bags and place them in refrigeration for an hour or more.

Serves 4 to 6 adults.

CHICKEN BREAST WITH PAPRIKA CREAM SAUCE

4 boneless, skinless chicken breast halves
pepper to taste
flour (or other coating) for dredging
4 tablespoons vegetable oil
2 tablespoons butter
1 cup chicken broth
⅔ cup heavy (whipping) cream
1 tablespoon paprika
5 green onions - 2 whole, 3 finely chopped

Trim about an inch off both the top and bottom of 3 of the green onions. Discard the end cuttings and chop the remaining parts into small pieces across their length. Set aside for later.

Trim the chicken breast halves of any excess fat. With a mallet flatten the meat into even cutlets. Don't strike the meat too hard or it will tear. This makes it harder to handle, and it will not look as nice. Pepper both sides of each cutlet according to your taste.

Set a wide skillet over medium high heat and add the vegetable oil. While the oil is heating, dredge the chicken in flour. Lay each cutlet carefully in the hot oil and cook until browned on each side, 3 to 4 minutes per side. I often substitute Golden Dipt brand, boxed, chicken coating mix for the flour. It gives a darker color to the coating, and has nice flavor.

When the chicken is browned and cooked so that the juices run clear when the meat is pierced, transfer it to a low oven, or to a heated plate. Don't cover the meat.

Pour off most of the oil in the skillet, but try to retain the browned bits of chicken and coating remaining in the pan. Set the pan back over medium high heat and deglaze the skillet by adding the chicken broth. Stir the broth while scraping the pan bottom to incorporate the browned bits into a pan sauce. Simmer the broth for a minute and then add the butter, cream, paprika, and half the chopped onions. Stir this sauce and bring it to a brisk simmer. Stir, cook, and reduce this sauce to about half its original volume.

Serve 2 breast halves per portion on a dinner plate. Pour some paprika cream sauce over each cutlet. Sprinkle with the remaining chopped green onion. Garnish each plate with a green onion cluster.

Serves 2.

BAYOU BREAST OF CHICKEN

4 boned & skinned chicken breast halves
2 links (6 inches each) chicken & apple sausage
1 can (29 ounces) tomato sauce
3 tablespoons finely chopped green pepper
3 tablespoons finely chopped onion
2 tablespoons butter
2 cloves garlic - minced
1 tablespoon brown sugar
1½ teaspoons cumin
3 tablespoons room temperature butter

Cajun Seasoning

½ teaspoon onion powder
½ teaspoon garlic powder
½ teaspoon white pepper
¼ teaspoon red pepper
½ teaspoon each black pepper, thyme
¼ teaspoon salt
½ teaspoon paprika

Sauté the green pepper & onion in 2 tablespoons butter for about 3 minutes. Add the minced garlic and cook 2 minutes more. Add the tomato sauce, brown sugar, and cumin. Bring the sauce to a simmer. Cook over low heat for at least 30 minutes.

Cook the sausage links in a skillet until just done. Set aside to cool.

With a mallet, pound the breast halves to ¼-inch thickness. Cut the sausage links into short lengths. Roll a piece of sausage in each breast half. Tuck the edges of the chicken towards the center as you roll up the sausage in the chicken fillet. Combine the Cajun seasoning ingredients in a shallow bowl. Roll each chicken and sausage roll in the room temperature butter. Next roll them in the Cajun seasoning to coat.

In a very hot and dry black iron skillet, cook the chicken rolls until blackened on all sides. Turn the heat down a little and add a half cup of water to the skillet. Cover quickly and cook for about 5 minutes to finish cooking the chicken.

Serve the chicken in pools of the seasoned tomato sauce.

Serves 4.

ORIENTAL STUFFED CHICKEN BREASTS

8 boneless breast halves
1½ cup raw white rice
3 cups chicken broth
1 cup beef broth
1 cup Kikkoman Soy Sauce
2 tablespoons honey
1 large bunch green onions - chopped
3 tablespoons minced parsley
2 stalks celery - chopped fine
1 can (12 ounces) mushroom stems & pieces
3 tablespoons butter
4 individual ramekin baking dishes

In a sauce pan combine 3 cups chicken broth, 1 cup beef broth, 1 cup Kikkoman, and 2 tablespoons honey. Stir and bring to a simmer.

Cook the 1½ cups of rice in 3½ cups of the above mixture (add 1 tablespoon butter to the broth mixture) over low heat for about 12 - 15 minutes or until rice is about three-quarters done. Remove from heat and add the minced parsley, chopped celery, chopped green onion, and mushroom stems and pieces. Stir together.

Grease or butter your ramekins. Layer each ramekin as follows: 1 breast half (lightly pounded), about ½ cup of the partially cooked rice and vegetable mixture, and top with another lightly pounded breast half. Smear the top breast half with butter. Pour about ¼ cup of the broth mixture over and around the layered chicken and rice and cover loosely with foil.

Bake 45 minutes at 350. Check the ramekins at about 30 minutes to see that they are still moist. Add more broth if needed. Remove foil from top and check for doneness (breast meat should be white throughout and the juices should be clear). When done, remove foil and finish under broiler to desired doneness.

Thicken remaining broth with a little cornstarch and cold water to serve as gravy at the table.

Serves 4.

CHICKEN ENCHILADAS

4 small boneless chicken breasts
1 package (8 ounces) cream cheese
½ cup sour cream
minced jalapena peppers or green chilies - to taste
2 teaspoons cumin
8 flour (white) tortillas
3 cups grated cojack cheese
enchilada sauce (recipe follows)

In a wide skillet pour water to cover the chicken breasts and bring to a boil over high heat. Reduce the heat to a simmer and poach the chicken for about 10 minutes, or until just done. Turn the meat once. Set the meat aside to cool.

Allow the cream cheese to come to room temperature. Place it in a large bowl with the sour cream, cumin, and peppers or chilies. Stir to blend.

Cut the cooked chicken into bite-sized pieces and fold the chopped meat into the cream cheese mixture.

Place about 4 tablespoons of the mixture on each of the tortillas. Sprinkle a little cojack cheese over each portion. Roll up the tortillas as per package instructions. Place them seam side down on a large, lightly greased, baking sheet. Top each rolled tortilla with a small amount of enchilada sauce and bake at 350 degrees for about 20 minutes. Refresh the sauce on each tortilla by adding a little to each portion.

Sprinkle each tortilla with cojack cheese and allow it to melt before serving. Serve extra sauce in bowl on the table.

Enchilada Sauce

1 can (28 ounces) tomato sauce
minced jalapeno peppers or green chilies to taste
½ teaspoon each - cumin, oregano, and sugar
1 teaspoon chili sauce

Heat the tomato sauce in a pan and season it with the peppers or chilies, cumin, oregano, sugar, and chili powder. Bring the sauce to a simmer and cook for 15 minutes. Taste and adjust seasonings and simmer for 10 minutes more.

Serves 4.

FRIED CHICKEN BASICS

Heat enough peanut or vegetable oil in a large skillet to submerge the pieces of chicken to the half way point.

Use a large enough skillet to accommodate the pieces of chicken to be fried without crowding them to the point where they are difficult to turn. Use two or more skillets if necessary.

Heat the oil to medium-high or to the point where the oil sizzles very noticeably when you lower the tip of a piece of chicken into it. If you can't get this reaction, heat the oil longer or turn it up. Try it again before you commit your batch of chicken to the oil.

If you really want to be a fried chicken purist buy a 10- or- 12-inch black iron skillet. Coat it with oil in which chicken has previously been fried and bake it at 275 degrees for 3 hours. When cool, wipe it out with paper towels. For the rest of its career use it solely for the purpose of frying chicken. Wash it sparingly with only the mildest mix of water and detergents.

Wash chicken pieces under cold water and blot dry with paper towels. Lay the chicken out on waxed paper (at this point I skin the chicken pieces by hand; skinning the chicken is a matter of personal preference). Salt and pepper the chicken generously. Turn each piece over and repeat the seasoning. Next, coat the chicken with Golden Dipt Crispy Chicken Frying Mix. Pour about a cup of this coating in a plastic bag and coat two pieces at a time by closing the bag and tossing the chicken pieces until they are covered. It takes very little time to coat the chicken so the chicken can be put in the oil two at a time as they are coated.

Fry the chicken for 5 minutes and then turn each piece and fry it for 5 minutes more on the other side. Turn the chicken about every five minutes and change the position of the pieces in the pan. The center of your pan will be hotter than the perimeter. Changing the position of the pieces of chicken will help achieve even browning and degree of doneness. Fry the chicken for a total of 25 minutes. Blot it on paper towels. Allow it to cool for a few minutes before serving.

Boneless chicken cooks much faster than bone-in chicken. If frying boneless pieces of breasts with bone-in thighs, put the breast meat in the pan after the thighs have cooked for 10 minutes. Then finish the skillet of chicken for 15 more minutes.

The "Southern" method for frying chicken calls for about 10 minutes of browning in a hot open skillet of oil. The heat is then turned to medium-low and the pan is covered for about 45 minutes (some "Southern" style recipes call for the addition of a few tablespoons of water before the pan is covered). After 45 minutes the heat is turned up and the pan uncovered for a 10-minute crisping period. I've used this method with pleasing results. I personally don't feel there is a gain in quality for the extra time expended so I use the 25-minute over medium-high heat method.

Chicken wings fried over medium-high heat cook in about 12 - 15 minutes.

CHICKEN MARSALA

4 boneless, skinless, chicken breast halves
black pepper to taste
flour for dredging
4 tablespoons vegetable oil
4 tablespoons butter
⅓ cup Marsala wine
¼ cup chicken broth
1 tablespoon minced fresh parsley

Use a meat mallet to pound the chicken into uniformly flat cutlets. Do not pound the breast halves so hard that you tear the meat.

Sprinkle both sides with a little pepper, and dredge lightly with flour or Golden Dipt brand chicken coating.

Heat the vegetable oil over high heat in a wide skillet. Add the chicken cutlets and cook them until lightly browned on both sides, 3 to 4 minutes per side. Transfer the cutlets to a warm platter.

Pour off the fat from the skillet. Return the skillet to the range over medium high heat. Add the chicken broth to the skillet and stir with a wooden utensil, scraping up and dissolving any browned bits in the skillet. Add the butter to the skillet. As soon as the butter melts add the Marsala wine and about half the parsley. Stir the pan sauce again with a wooden utensil.

Return the chicken to the skillet. Cook the chicken in the pan sauce for about 5 minutes, or until the sauce reduces to the consistency of a thin gravy. Turn the cutlets once while cooking.

To serve, place two cutlets on a plate. Drizzle a little pan sauce over the meat, and sprinkle a little minced parsley over all.

Serves 2 adults.

CHICKEN PICATA

2 boneless chicken breast halves per guest served
salt & pepper
flour for dredging
¼ cup olive oil
4 tablespoons butter
⅓ cup dry white wine
⅓ cup chicken broth
juice of one lemon
minced parsley
lemon garnish

Pound boneless breast halves lightly to make the fillets an even thickness (a little less than ½ inch). Salt and pepper each breast half and dredge each seasoned fillet on both sides in flour.

Heat a large skillet. Add the oil and heat to medium-high heat. Sauté the chicken until brown on both sides. When brown, transfer the fillets to a warm platter.

Pour off the oil from the pan. Reheat the pan and add and melt the butter. When the butter is melted and heated to about medium, add the white wine, chicken broth, lemon juice and parsley. Stir the liquid ingredients and add the browned chicken.

Cook the breasts and pan sauce until the sauce reaches a nice gravy-like consistency. Place the breasts on a serving plate and pour sauce over them. Garnish with a lemon slice and a little more parsley.

■ Pat food dry with paper towels to remove surface moisture before coating with breading or batter. Excess surface moisture will burst from the food surface when exposed to hot oil. Much of the coating will also leave the food surface. It pays to take this extra step.

CHICKEN STIR FRY

¾ pound, raw, boneless, cut-up chicken
1 large carrot - skinned and sliced thin
1 bunch green onions - bias cut
1 large stem broccoli - bias cut
15 - 20 snow peas
cauliflower florets
1 small yellow squash - sliced
1 red pepper - cut julienne style
6 large mushrooms - sliced
peanut oil as needed
Kikkoman soy sauce
garlic powder - optional
1 cup chicken broth
sesame oil
cornstarch for thickening - optional

Clean and cut your ingredients and lay them out near your heat source. Heat your wok or skillet over medium-high heat. Add enough peanut oil to coat your intended ingredients, about ⅓ cup. Use wooden utensils, if possible, for safety sake and to protect your pan.

Add your ingredients in order of their density of texture with the thickest and most dense products first in line. In this case the broccoli and cauliflower go first. Stir. Add the carrots. Stir. Add the chicken and stir. If you feel you need a little more peanut oil to coat your foods add it now a little at a time. Stir the pan as you add the oil. Cook for a few minutes and add the snow peas and red pepper. Stir again. Cook and stir for a short time and add the green onions, yellow squash, and mushrooms. Stir. Add about ½ cup chicken broth reserving the other ½ cup in case you feel you need it later to change the texture of the stir fry.

Season your stir fry with about 3 tablespoons Kikkoman and 2 tablespoons sesame oil. Stir to distribute. Add some garlic powder if you like. Continue to cook and stir until the chicken is done and the vegetables are crisp tender. Thicken a few minutes before serving with a little cornstarch and water if you like.

Serves 4 to 6.

POLYNESIAN GRILLED CHICKEN BREASTS

½ bottle (5 ounces) Lea & Perrin's White Wine Worcestershire Sauce
1 tablespoon Herlocher's Dipping Mustard
1 teaspoon dried tarragon
4 to 6 chicken breast halves

Combine the White Wine Worcestershire Sauce, dipping mustard, and tarragon in a bowl and stir. Pound the breast halves lightly on a flat surface to make them into even cutlets. Add the flattened chicken to the marinade and let stand at room temperature for 30 minutes. Or cover and refrigerate for 2 hours or longer.

After 30 minutes the chicken is ready to grill or sauté in melted butter and a few tablespoons of the marinade. When grilling, boil the remaining marinade for a few minutes. Then it can be used for a basting sauce at the grill. You may need to add a little more sauce and mustard to add more volume.

Serves 2 or 3 adults.

GRILLED GAME HENS

2 Cornish hens - thawed
¼ pound butter or margarine
¼ cup vinegar
1 teaspoon paprika
1 teaspoon pepper
1 teaspoon salt
1 teaspoon poultry seasoning
2 teaspoons brown sugar
2 tablespoons ketchup

Melt the butter in a sauce pan over medium heat. Add the next 7 ingredients and stir to blend. Simmer the sauce for 10 minutes and remove from heat.

While the sauce cools to room temperature split each game hen by cutting it lengthwise. Cut with a large sharp knife or with kitchen shears. Be careful to cut closely along side the breast and back bone. Rinse the halved birds under cold water.

In a shallow baking pan or gallon size zip lock bag, marinate the birds in the barbecue sauce for about 45 minutes at room temperature, or for a few hours under refrigeration.

Preheat the oven to 375 degrees. Also preheat a gas or charcoal grill. Boil the marinade for basting. Put the halved birds on the grill. Because the sauce is oil (butter) based, it will tend to cause flare ups on the grill. For this reason use medium heat and a height of about 6 inches from the heat source. Grill each side until it is nicely browned. The cooking time will vary from grill to grill. About 8 - 10 minutes per side is about right. Baste the birds as they cook.

When the birds are nicely colored, baste them with more sauce and finish them in the oven in a covered baking dish. Check them to be sure they remain moist. Add more sauce as needed. They will need a cooking time of about 40 minutes.

Serve over wild rice. Serves 4.

MEDITERRANEAN GAME HENS

2 whole cornish game hens (about 3-3½ pounds total)
¾ cup olive oil
½ teaspoon salt
1 teaspoon dried basil
¼ teaspoon oregano
½ teaspoon celery salt
½ teaspoon paprika
2 tablespoons fresh minced parsley
about 30 twists of fresh ground pepper

Thaw game hens. Split the birds by cutting along and right beside the breast and back bone with a chef's knife or kitchen shears. Trim the halved birds of hanging skin.

Mix the marinade using the latter 9 ingredients above. Place the marinade and the halved game hens in a gallon-sized zip lock plastic bag. Marinate the birds for an hour at room temperature or for several hours in refrigeration.

Bake the game hens on a rack in a shallow baking pan for about 45 minutes in a 350 degree oven. Pour the excess marinade in the bottom of the baking pan. Use it to baste the birds a few times while cooking.

The game hens will also grill nicely over moderate coals. Turn often and baste with marinade which you have cooked at a low boil in a sauce pan for about 5 minutes.

Serves 4.

■ After selecting a recipe, lay out all the ingredients so that you know you have what you need before you begin. It's also a good idea to lay out tools, cookware, and serving pieces.

BARBECUE SAUSAGE WITH LEEKS & PEPPERS

8 sausage links (3 ounces each; suggest Italian)
2 red bell peppers
2 green peppers
1 bunch leeks
6 tablespoons butter
bamboo or metal skewers

I mention butter in the ingredient list because it is my choice to precook the peppers and leeks in a few tablespoons butter over medium heat in a sauté pan. You may choose to microwave, steam, or boil them. Just about any method is fine.

Precook the sausage to the point where it is just done. Bake, poach, boil, fry, or microwave.

Cut the stem ends out of the red and green peppers and shake out the seeds. Cut the peppers into inch-wide strips vertically. Trim all of the white, raised ribbing from the inside seams. Precook the pepper strips until they are crisp tender. They should hold their form after cooking and not be limp.

Cut the root end from a large leek (you may need two leeks). Cut the stalk of the leek off at about 5 inches from the cut base. Now slice the stalk of leek in half lengthwise. Separate the leek into layers and thoroughly wash each piece under cold running water. Precook the leeks until just done (taste to test). Save the upper section of the leeks. Chop them and sauté them in butter. They make a great accessory to home fried potatoes.

Fit each sausage into a few concave leek sections. Now, using two skewers set about an inch apart, skewer a green pepper slice, a red pepper slice, and a leek covered sausage. Repeat as room on the skewers permits.

Grill over medium hot coals until marked by the grill and heated through. Serve on a bed of yellow rice, or over home fries mixed with the chopped leeks from above the stalk cutting.

Serves 4.

■ When the waiter brings the bottle of wine to the table to be tested for approval, do the following: Hold the test glass away from you and inspect it visually. The wine should be free of grape and/or cork sediment. Gently swirl the wine in the glass a few times and then smell it at close range. It should have no musky or vinegar-like aroma. Finally, taste the wine. It should taste like wine and be free of any vinegar like flavor.

BONELESS PORK BARBECUE EXPRESS

This recipe works with chops, ribs, country style ribs, small pork roasts, tenderloins, or pork fish. A small adjustment in cooking times is needed for larger cuts of pork.

3 pounds pork fish (tenderloin)
1 cup bottled chili sauce
⅔ cup ketchup
¼ cup lemon juice
2 tablespoons brown sugar
2 teaspoons Worcestershire sauce
½ teaspoon garlic salt
a few drops - bottled hot pepper sauce, or more to taste
¼ cup water

Place the clean gasket in the lid of your pressure cooker. Hold the lid up to the light so you can sight through the steam vent to see that it is clear of any obstruction.

Spray the kettle section of the cooker with Pam. Put the sauce ingredients, the chili sauce, ketchup, lemon juice, brown sugar, Worcestershire sauce, garlic salt, bottled hot pepper sauce, and water in the sprayed kettle section.

Trim the pork fish of any fat or surface tissue. Cut each fish into 2-inch lengths. Pound the pork pieces into cutlets with a meat mallet. Place the pork cutlets in the sauce in the kettle. Turn to coat.

Fasten the lid to the kettle and place the "jiggle" control over the steam vent. Place the cooker over high heat. When the control starts to "hiss" and jiggle, turn the heat to low. Begin timing cook time at this point. The control should rock gently and steadily, or jiggle sporadically, 3 to 4 times a minute, at the new low setting. Cook for 10 minutes.

After 10 minutes relieve the pressure in the pot by running cold tap water over the lid of the cooker for about 3 minutes. Lift the jiggle control off the steam vent with a set of tongs. Open the lid and serve. Serves 3 to 4.

Save any extra sauce. Add ½ cup melted butter and some more bottled hot sauce and use it to coat cooked chicken wing sections. It makes outrageously good Buffalo style hot wings!

PORK TENDERLOIN WITH EGGPLANT & CHEESE

Seasoned Tomato Sauce

1 pork steak (6 ounces)
2 tablespoons vegetable oil
1 can (15 ounces) tomato sauce
¼ cup water
1 can (16 ounces) whole tomatoes - crushed
⅓ cup water
1 tablespoon fresh minced parsley
1 tablespoon grated parmesan cheese
1 medium bay leaf
¼ teaspoon each oregano, onion powder
½ teaspoon garlic powder
¼ teaspoon basil
1 tablespoon brown sugar
salt & pepper to taste

In a wide (8 to 10 inches) deep skillet heat 2 tablespoons oil over medium high heat. Fry the pork steak in the hot oil until well browned on both sides.

While the pork steak fries crush the whole tomatoes in a bowl. Rinse the tomato can with ⅓ cup water and save that tomato water. Add the tomato sauce to the bowl and rinse that can with about ¼ cup water. Add that water to the bowl. Then add to the bowl the parsley, parmesan cheese, bay leaf, oregano, onion powder, garlic powder, basil, brown sugar, salt and pepper. Stir to blend.

When the pork steak has browned on both sides remove it and set it aside. Turn the heat to medium and deglaze the skillet with the reserved tomato water. Scrape the pan bottom while the tomato water simmers in the skillet. After just a few minutes add the seasoned tomato mixture in the bowl to the skillet. Add the pork steak back to the skillet. Allow the sauce to come to a brisk simmer. Stir the mixture frequently. Cook at a brisk simmer for 30 to 45 minutes or until the sauce thickens to the consistency of spaghetti sauce. Taste and correct seasonings when the sauce thickens.

While the sauce is cooking, you can prepare the pork and the eggplant.

PORK, EGGPLANT, & CHEESE INGREDIENTS

1 pork fish tenderloin (12 to 16 ounces)
1 medium eggplant
3 beaten eggs
1 cup flour
2 cups Italian seasoned bread crumbs
6 tablespoons butter
6 tablespoons vegetable oil
2 cups shredded provolone cheese
1/2 cup grated parmesan cheese
salt & pepper

Trim the pork fish free of any "silver" tissue. Cut into 4 equal pieces. Pound these pieces into flat cutlets with a meat mallet. Salt and pepper the cutlets on both sides and set them aside on waxed paper.

Skin the eggplant enough to get eight ¼-inch skinless round slices from the vegetable.

Set a skillet over medium heat with 3 tablespoons butter and 3 tablespoons vegetable oil. Dredge the eggplant slices in flour. Coat each slice, one at a time with the beaten eggs and then with the seasoned bread crumbs. As soon as each slice is coated put it in the hot skillet and brown it on both sides. Allow the eggplant to drain on paper towels.

Drain off the butter and oil from the skillet and add 3

tablespoons (each) of new butter and oil to the skillet. Repeat the flour, egg, and bread crumb coating process with the pork cutlets and brown each of them on both sides also.

Place a thin layer of the seasoned tomato sauce in the bottom of a shallow baking pan, or into 4 individual baking dishes. Layer a cutlet of pork, shredded provolone cheese, grated parmesan cheese, 2 breaded eggplant slices (layered like roof shingles), and another thin layer of sauce. Don't use so much sauce on top that lots of breaded product does not show on the top and sides.

Bake in individual dishes, or in a shallow pan uncovered at 350 degrees for 30 minutes. Top with a little more grated cheese and minced fresh parsley just before serving. Pass remaining sauce in a bowl.

Serves 4 hungry adults.

GRILLED SPARE RIBS

3 to 4 pounds pork loin back ribs
1 cup bottled chili sauce
⅔ cup ketchup
¼ cup lemon juice
2 tablespoons brown sugar
2 teaspoons Worcestershire sauce
½ teaspoon garlic salt
a few drops bottled hot pepper sauce, or more to taste

Place ribs in a shallow baking pan. Pre-heat oven to 350 degrees.

While the oven is warming, mix all the sauce ingredients together in a bowl. Brush the ribs with the sauce on all sides. Place the ribs in the pan with the meaty side facing up. Bake at 350 degrees, uncovered, for 1 hour. Check them occasionally for excessive browning. Cover the ribs loosely with foil, if necessary, to prevent them from becoming too dark. When done the ribs are ready to be finished on the grill. Simply cook them until they develop a nice outdoor grill color, and until they are heated through. Baste the ribs as they cook on the grill.

Serves 3 to 4 adults.

KOSHER SALAMI & SHARP CHEESE SANDWICHES

1 tube (12 ounces) of Kosher Salami
8 ounces very sharp cheese
¼ cup prepared mustard
⅓ cup Miracle Whip
¼ cup chopped onion
2 tablespoons sweet pickle relish

Use an old fashioned, counter mounted, hand cranked, food grinder to grind the salami and cheese. An electric food processor will also work. Be careful to coarse chop, not puree the ingredients. Place the ground meat and cheese in a bowl. Add other ingredients and mix. Serve hot on small rolls for appetizers or in hot dog rolls for sandwiches. Cover the foil while heating.

These sandwiches freeze nicely for up to 6 months. Reheat them at 350 degrees for 25 minutes.

Makes 8 sandwiches.

■ White fleshed seafood (shrimp, lobster, whitefish, scallops, etc.) are properly cooked when all the opaque shade is gone, and the flesh is pure white throughout. Cut a large piece to check. If it's all white inside, it's done. Every time!

PORK FRANCAISE

1 very large, or 2 small pork fish (tenderloin)
salt & pepper
flour for dredging
2 large eggs
5 tablespoons butter
⅓ cup Sauterne wine
1 large red delicious apple, cored and chopped
1 large golden delicious apple cored and chopped
1 tablespoon fresh minced parsley

Trim all the white tissue from the pork fish, that is trim it so that it is all bare meat. Cut it across its length into 8 equal sized pieces.

Use a meat mallet to pound the cut pork into thin cutlets. Lightly salt and pepper the meat on both sides. Dredge each cutlet in flour.

Beat the eggs in a bowl with 2 tablespoons water. Heat the butter in a wide skillet over medium heat. You may use higher heat if you choose to use clarified butter. Dip the floured pork cutlets in the egg wash. When fully covered transfer them to the skillet. Cook the meat until lightly browned on both sides. Add the wine to the skillet and swirl the pan to mix the wine and butter. Sprinkle a little parsley over all and cook the pork in the sauce for about a minute.

Place the red and yellow chopped apples in the skillet. Sprinkle a little more parsley in the pan and cook the meat with the apples until the meat is well heated again. The meat can be tested by piercing it with a knife. It is done if the juices run clear, not pink.

Serve 2 cutlets per portion. Spoon some chopped apples over and around the meat and drizzle some of the wine and butter sauce over each portion. Sprinkle a fresh pinch of minced parsley over all for a nice presentation.

PORK WITH RED PEPPERS & PINEAPPLE

1 can (8 ounces) crushed pineapple, undrained
2 cloves garlic, halved
1 teaspoon ground ginger
2 tablespoons red wine vinegar
3 tablespoons soy sauce
½ cup ketchup
½ cup hoisin sauce
3 pounds boneless pork leg or shoulder, cut into 1½ inch cubes
3 large red peppers, seeded and cut into 1½ inch squares
1 large pineapple, cored and peeled, and cut into 1½ inch cubes
bamboo or metal skewers

In a blender or food processor, combine canned pineapple with juice, garlic, ginger, vinegar, soy, hoisin, and ketchup. Blend until mixed well.

Pour the mixture into a large bowl and mix in the pork cubes. Cover and marinate overnight in the refrigerator. Stir the pork occasionally.

This and other similar recipes are a lot easier to handle if you take the time to precook the meat. You can simmer the pork in its marinade in an open skillet. The meat can be baked, covered, in the oven. It can also be cooked in a microwave oven. Whatever method you choose, the object is to cook the meat until it is just done. The skewers will go on the grill for just enough time to color them with grill marking, and to heat them to a hot serving temperature. This will be about 10-12 minutes.

When the meat is to be paired with a densely textured vegetable like red pepper, then I think the vegetable could stand a little precooking also.

Once the initial cooking is done, the skewers may be threaded, red pepper, cubed fresh pineapple, pork, and repeat until you come to within an inch of the end of the skewer. They are now ready to be finished on the grill.

If you want to serve the marinade as a dipping sauce, be sure to cook it at a simmer for about 15 minutes. Add water as necessary to control texture.

Serves 4.

■ When pan frying or sautéing, heat the pan while it is dry. Then add the oil or butter. Allow a few minutes for either to heat. Then add the food and continue cooking. Foods will not stick as readily.

STOVE TOP "BAKED" HAM

Here's an easy way to prepare ham. You'll need a large pot with a tight fitting lid and a rack on which to set the ham. The rack should stand at least an inch above the bottom of the pot so that you can add enough liquid at the start that you won't have to add liquid frequently as you cook (in this case steam) the ham.

Purchase a boneless, pre-cooked, ham that is large enough to serve the intended number of guests and small enough to fit your covered pot.

A five-pound boneless ham will serve 8 people after shrinkage.

3 cans (6 ounces each) of unsweetened pineapple juice
1 1/2 cups Marsala Wine
1 – 4-6 pound boneless ham

Trim a thin slice off one side of the ham to create a flat surface on which the ham will rest while cooking. Or, if using a half ham, slice it in half vertically. Pour the three cans of pineapple juice and the Marsala wine in the pot. Set the rack in place in the pot. It should rest just above the surface of the juice and wine. Place the ham on the rack and fit the lid in place.

Bring the pot to a boil to create steam and back the heat off to a steady simmer which creates constant steam. The steam should be steady but not violent.

That's about all there is to it. Steam the ham for about two hours, longer if possible. Check the pot on occasion to make sure it does not steam dry. Add water when necessary to keep the liquid at a depth of at least 1 inch. Baste the ham two to three times an hour. Your pan liquid will thicken and intensify in flavor. Serve it as an accessory sauce at the table. Be sure to taste it to see if it needs to be sweetened.

Rest the ham for 15 minutes before slicing. Your ham will be well-seasoned and moist. I think you'll also enjoy the texture of the ham.

STUFFED PORK ROAST

⅓ cup finely chopped onion
⅓ cup finely chopped green pepper
2 cloves garlic, minced
1 teaspoon salt
1 teaspoon ground red pepper
1 teaspoon ground black pepper
1 3-4 pound boneless pork loin roast

For stuffing, in a mixing bowl combine onion, green pepper, garlic, salt, red pepper, and black pepper. Mix well.

Cut 12 to 14 deep slits, 1 inch wide, randomly around pork roast in the side opposite of the fatted side. Using your fingers, stuff the slits with some of the stuffing. Place roast, fat side up, on a rack in a shallow roasting pan. Rub remaining stuffing mixture over roast.

Roast pork, uncovered, in a 325 degree oven for 2½ to 3 hours or until an instant thermometer registers 170 degrees. Let pork roast rest on the counter for 15 minutes before carving.

Serves 8 - 10.

TERIYAKI PORK SPARE RIBS

5 pounds pork spare ribs
¾ cup sugar
¾ cup water
1½ cups chicken broth
1 bottle (10 ounces) Kikkoman soy sauce
½ teaspoon powdered ginger
½ teaspoon garlic powder
2 tablespoons dry sherry (optional)

Prepare a simple syrup by bringing the ¾ cup water to a boil. Slowly stir in the ¾ cup sugar. Stir until the sugar dissolves. Set aside to cool.

Begin preparing a teriyaki sauce with this in mind. Save some of each ingredient for taste adjustment later.

In a sauce pan mix 1 cup chicken broth, ½ cup simple syrup, and ½ cup Kikkoman soy sauce. Bring the mixture to a low boil. Season with half of the ginger, garlic, and sherry if used. Taste the sauce. We want a pleasing sweet soy flavor. Adjust with simple syrup if not sweet enough. Use the soy sauce and chicken broth if it is too sweet for your liking. The garlic and ginger should be noticeable but not dominant.

Thicken the sauce with corn starch and water to a gravy consistency when the flavor is correct for you.

You may separate the pork ribs before or after cooking. I usually cut them into 2 bone portions prior to cooking because I tend to serve the ribs as appetizers.

Place the ribs in a roasting pan and sprinkle them with a generous amount of Kikkoman soy sauce. Add a half cup water to the pan and cook the ribs uncovered in a 375 degree oven for 30 minutes. Turn the ribs; add a little water and soy sauce if needed to keep the pan moist. Cook for 30 minutes more.

Next baste the ribs with teriyaki sauce, add a little water to the pan if needed (again), cover with foil and cook for 30 minutes at 325 degrees.

Drain the grease from the pan. Baste the ribs again with teriyaki sauce. Cook for about 20 minutes, uncovered.

Two cautions. Because of the dark color and the sugar content of the teriyaki sauce, the ribs should be checked occasionally for moisture. This is a dish that needs frequent checking. Serve ribs with bowls of teriyaki sauce.

Serves 4.

YUCATAN PORK & CHICKEN KABOBS

1 pound cooked smoked sausage
4 boneless chicken breast halves
1 medium sized zucchini
1 medium sized yellow squash
1 large red bell pepper

Marinade & Basting Sauce

Make 2 batches of sauce, or double the following ingredients.

½ cup Heinz Hamburger Relish
¼ cup water
1 teaspoon brown sugar
1 tablespoon McCormick's Mexican seasoning

Cut the smoked sausage into inch-long pieces. Cut the chicken breast halves into similar size pieces. Cut the zucchini and yellow squash into ½-inch circles. Core and seed the red pepper and cut it into 1-inch squares.

Mix the first marinade sauce by whisking the ingredients together in a bowl. Set this sauce aside to use as a basting sauce for grilling the kabobs.

Mix another batch of sauce. Use ¾ cup of water to produce a thinner version. Use the sauce to sauté the chicken pieces in a skillet. When the chicken is just done remove the sauce and meat from the heat and allow it to cool. When near room temperature place the chicken and sauce in a bowl or plastic bag to marinate for an hour at room temperature, or for 2 or more hours in refrigeration.

Boil for 5 minutes, then save the marinade sauce as a condiment to serve with the finished product.

Blanch, or cook until crisp tender, the peppers, zucchini, and squash. You can microwave, steam, or boil the vegetables. Be sure to just cook them lightly.

Now thread the chicken, cut sausage, and vegetables on skewers. Place the skewers on a moderately hot grill and baste them with the basting sauce. Turn and baste them frequently.

Cook the kabobs until they begin to become grill marked, and are heated through.

Simmer the marinade and serve with the grilled kabobs.

Serves 4.

TURKEY TALK

Don't settle for chicken gravy to serve with your turkey. Use a turkey gravy mix from the local supermarket, or better yet, use a commercial turkey flavor base to make a rich broth for gravy making.

Try roasting your turkey breast side down. Steady the fire with wadded aluminum foil on either side or with metal utensils. The breast meat will be very moist when the turkey is done.

I like to smear the skin of the turkey with butter before seasoning with poultry seasoning. Use a plastic sandwich bag like a glove to rub room temperature butter over the surface of the bird.

Always roast poultry in a preheated oven. Roast at 325 to 350 degrees for about 25 minutes per pound or until the internal temperature reads 180 degrees for a bone in bird or 170 degrees for a boneless turkey. Boneless turkeys require about 35 minutes per pound cooking time.

I prefer to put about a cup of water or broth in the cavity of a roasting turkey. I find that this yields moist meat. Conventional stuffing inside the bird tastes good but absorbs moisture from the meat. I prefer to make stuffing separately from the bird and moisten it with rich turkey broth.

A rule of thumb for poultry is that whole birds yield 50 percent of total starting weight as edible meat after cooking. Use this rule when selecting your turkey for the number of guests you intend to serve. Twelve ounces of cooked turkey per person is usually plenty. A twelve-pound raw turkey will yield six pounds of cooked meat and will serve eight diners. Buy a larger bird if you want leftovers.

Buy fresh birds with "sell by" dates that give you a few

days grace beyond your intended cook date. If something happens to disrupt your plans you'll still have time to cook the bird without concern for freshness.

Freeze cooked turkey meat up to three days after cooking. Always mark and date meats and other food products before freezing. A freezer list posted on the side of your refrigerator or freezer will help you efficiently store and consume your leftovers. Cooked poultry may be frozen for up to six months. Frozen raw poultry can be kept longer. I have a basic distrust of any product frozen for more than six months and try to prepare them within that time limit.

BARBECUE TURKEY TENDERLOINS

1½ cups (or a 12 oz. can) lemon-lime soda
¼ cup Kikkoman soy sauce
¼ cup vegetable oil
2 tablespoons prepared horseradish
1 teaspoon garlic powder
3 turkey tenderloins - halved

In a gallon-sized zip lock bag combine the lemon-lime soda, soy sauce, oil, horseradish, and garlic powder. Add the turkey tenderloins. Seal and refrigerate for 2 or more hours.

When ready to cook, remove turkey tenderloins from the bag and place on a hot grill. Discard the marinade. Grill the turkey 5 to 6 minutes per side, or until it is no longer pink in the center.

■ Gallon-sized zip lock plastic bags are great for marinating meats. Place the meat and marinade in the bag. Squeeze out the excess air and seal them tightly. Place on a large plate. To turn the meat, simply turn the bag.

BONELESS ROAST TURKEY

Many of us have been eating more turkey in recent years. I hope you'll try this boneless variety of turkey. It features some advantages that I think you will appreciate.

You may want to serve your family a boneless roast turkey or two before you feature it for a traditional holiday meal. There's a lot of tradition associated with the major holidays and one of those is the sight of a conventional roast turkey with the bones and legs attached.

My family prefers the boneless variety, because they feel the boneless bird has a better texture and more flavor. They also like the ease of handling when going for leftovers.

The boneless turkey is not a pressed meat product. It is an actual turkey that has been boned, defatted, rolled, and then netted. They range in size from 4 - 6 lbs. and are all meat. You cook them exactly like you would a bone in bird except you don't have the option of stuffing them. An average-sized boneless turkey will thaw in cold water in three hours. To cook just remove the outer wrappings. Roast on a rack over water or broth in a 350 degree oven for 35-40 minutes per pound or until internal temperature reaches 165-170 degrees F. Baste occasionally and cover with a loose foil tent when the turkey browns sufficiently. Rest 15 minutes before serving. After resting, cut and gently remove the net. Slice the roast turkey across its length in serving-sized pieces. The ration of white and dark meat is the same as a conventional roast turkey.

Another advantage to the boneless variety of turkey is its size. It requires less than half the storage and oven space than a conventional turkey yielding the same amount of meat. It's also the easiest bird you'll ever carve. No bones to cut around, and no messy carcass to handle.

TURKEY MARSALA

2 turkey tenderloins, about 2 pounds
salt and pepper
flour for dredging
5 tablespoons butter or margarine
½ cup Marsala wine
½ cup chicken broth
2 tablespoons finely chopped parsley

Slice the turkey across the length into ½ cutlets. Pound the cutlets lightly with a mallet taking care not to tear the meat. Sprinkle with salt and pepper and dredge in flour.

Heat the vegetable oil in a wide skillet. When it is quite hot add the turkey cutlets (A light sprinkling of paprika improves the color of the turkey cutlets). If you have more cutlets than your pan can accommodate, cook them in two batches. Start with half the oil and add oil as needed as you cook the second batch. Cook the turkey until just lightly browned on both sides, 3-4 minutes per side. Transfer the turkey to a warm platter.

Pour off the excess oil in the skillet. Turn the heat to medium. Add the chicken broth to the skillet. Scrape the bottom of the skillet lightly to incorporate any browned bits. Cook for about 2 minutes. Add the butter, Marsala wine, and 1 tablespoon shopped parsley. Stir to mix.

Return the turkey to the skillet. Cook the pan sauce and turkey for a few minutes on each side. Shingle the cutlets in serving portions on plates. Drizzle some butter, broth, and wine sauce over each portion and sprinkle a little chopped parsley over the top.

Serves 4.

SEAFOOD TIDBITS

Canned crab meat, snow crab clusters, and Alaskan King Crab legs and meat are all precooked. You need only to season and heat to serving temperature unless they are combined with raw ingredients that need cooking.

Raw clams and oysters in the shell that are partially open may still be healthy enough to eat. Gently pinch their shells together. If they stay shut they are alive and can be cooked. If they reopen within a minute, throw them away.

To prepare littleneck clams for steaming, soak them in cold fresh water with cornmeal, (⅓ cup cornmeal per gallon water) for 2-3 hours. They will disgorge most or all sand particles from inside their shells. Scrub them under cold running water with a stiff brush before steaming.

Fresh fish, whether filleted or dressed, has no fish odor. Fish odor as we know it, is decaying fish. If fish has any trace of odor, it is on the verge of a quick decline. Leave it for the cats.

Fresh scallops do smell like scallops. Don't fear the mild aroma of scallops before purchase. Real scallops, as opposed to cuts of skate or shark, have a small piece of tissue attached to the side. This is where they were attached to their shell. Not every scallop has this tissue because some remain attached to the shell entirely. For authenticity, at least some scallops in a group or package should have this noticeable tissue.

A good guide for buying reliable quality shrimp is to purchase shrimp packed by packers located on the Gulf of Mexico. Some shrimp packed by foreign packers yields less desirable results after cooking.

Plan to purchase fish and shellfish for same day consumption. (This is not an absolute must, but it sure eliminates risk and results in the best quality at serving time.) Ask your dealer for his delivery days and make it clear to him that you want your order to arrive for your purchase and pick-up on a selected delivery day. He'll be glad to comply because your cooking results will be of top quality and will reflect well on his reputation as a supplier.

Local commercial restaurant suppliers carry seafood products not readily available at local markets. Use them to expand your seafood menu (rainbow trout, soft-shell crabs, red snapper, etc). Be prepared to purchase whole boxes (usually 5 lbs). It's unfair to expect them to disrupt their inventory systems by breaking individual boxes.

CRAB IMPERIAL

1 pound backfin crab meat
3 tablespoons butter
1 tablespoon flour
½ cup milk
1 tablespoon minced onion
1½ teaspoons Worcestershire sauce
2 slices white bread, cubed (crusts removed)
½ cup mayonnaise or salad dressing
juice of ½ lemon
½ teaspoon salt
½ teaspoon pepper
paprika

Remove any cartilage from crab meat.

In a medium sauce pan melt 1 tablespoon butter. Stir in 1 tablespoon flour and cook over medium-low heat for a few minutes while stirring to keep mixture smooth. Slowly add milk, again while stirring. Raise the heat to medium-high and stir mixture until it comes to a slow boil and thickens. Fold in onions (cooked or uncooked - if uncooked make sure they are minced fine), Worcestershire, and bread cubes. Set aside to cool. After cooling for about 10 minutes fold in mayonnaise, lemon juice, and salt & pepper.

In a skillet, melt remaining butter over medium heat. Cook the butter until lightly browned. Then add the crab meat and toss lightly. Add the crab and butter into the sauce mixture and fold gently to mix.

Put mixture in individual ramekins or a 1 quart casserole and sprinkle with paprika. Bake at 400 degrees until hot and bubbly (10-15 minutes).

Serves 4.

MARYLAND CRAB CAKES

1 pound backfin crab meat
¾ cup seasoned bread crumbs
1 large egg (beaten)
about ¼ cup mayonnaise
1 teaspoon Worcestershire sauce
2 teaspoons dijon-style mustard
1 tablespoon fresh minced parsley
½ teaspoon salt
¼ teaspoon pepper
Margarine, butter, or oil for frying

Remove any cartilage from crab meat.

In a bowl mix the bread crumbs, egg, mayonnaise, and seasonings. Add crab meat and mix gently but thoroughly. If mixture is too dry add a little mayonnaise. Shape into six cakes by hand.

Cook crab cakes in a skillet over medium heat with just enough butter or oil to prevent sticking. Cook about 5 minutes per side or until nicely browned.

Crab cakes can also be broiled or deep fried. When broiling set the rack about 6 inches from the broiler heat source. When deep frying cook until browned all over. Drain on paper towels.

Whichever cooking method you use, remember that the crab meat is already cooked before you mix it with the other ingredients. You just want to brown the crab cakes and heat them through.

Makes six 3½ – ounce crab cakes.

CRAB ROMANOFF

1 pound backfin crab meat
2 cups hot cooked rice
1 container (8 ounces) sour cream
1 container (8 ounces) small curd cottage cheese
2 tablespoons finely chopped green pepper
2 tablespoons chopped chives
1 tablespoon Worcestershire sauce
dash salt
⅛ teaspoon red cayenne pepper
2-3 dashes garlic powder
1 can (4 ounces) mushroom stems & pieces, drained
3 tablespoons grated American cheese
paprika for garnish

Remove any cartilage from crab meat.

In a large bowl mix rice, sour cream, cottage cheese, and seasonings. Add mushrooms and crab meat; mix gently but thoroughly.

Put mixture into a greased 2-quart casserole. Sprinkle top with cheese and a little paprika.

Bake at 350 degrees until hot and bubbly, about 20 minutes.

Serves 6.

LUAU ORANGE ROUGHY

4 orange roughy fillets (8 ounces each)
½ cup orange juice
4 tablespoons bottled chili sauce
2 tablespoons vegetable oil
2 tablespoons sesame oil
2 tablespoon Kikkoman soy sauce
2 tablespoon lemon juice
½ teaspoon pepper
2 tablespoons sesame seeds, toasted
colorful fruits for garnish

Toast the sesame seeds in a dry skillet over medium heat. Toast them to a color of light brown. Set them aside to finish the dish.

In a bowl combine the orange juice, catsup, vegetable and sesame oil, soy sauce, lemon juice, and pepper. Pour the mixture over the (thawed) fillets in a shallow baking dish. Cover and refrigerate 2 hours. Drain the fillets, reserving the marinade; Place the fish on a rimmed broiling pan and broil or bake in a 425 degree oven. Allow 5 minutes cooking time for each half inch of thickness. Brush with the marinade as it cooks. Sprinkle with the sesame seeds before serving.

Garnish each serving with colorful fruit for a nice serving presentation.

Serves 4.

CAJUN BLACKENED RED SNAPPER

4 (4 to 6 ounces each) red snapper fillets
¼ teaspoon onion powder
½ teaspoon garlic powder
½ teaspoon white pepper
½ teaspoon red cayenne pepper
½ teaspoon black pepper
½ teaspoon dried thyme
½ teaspoon seafood seasoning
¼ teaspoon salt
½ cup melted butter

Thaw fish if frozen.

In a small bowl combine the dry spices.

Heat a large black iron (or thick aluminum) skillet over high heat. The skillet should be dry. When the skillet is very hot, brush each fillet with melted butter. Coat both sides with the seasoning mixture.

Add the seasoned fillets to the skillet. Cook uncovered about 3 minutes. Drizzle the top side of the fillets with the remaining butter, then turn them. Cook for about 3 minutes more. Serve when the fillets flake easily with a fork. Thicker fillets will require a little more time.

Serves 4.

■ To test to see if cooking oil is hot enough to begin frying or deep-frying, place just the tip of a piece of food in the oil. If you see a volatile and immediate reaction of tiny bubbles in the oil, then the oil is ready for frying. If you see little or no reaction, the oil is not hot enough. Continue heating the oil, and test again in a few minutes.

CANADIAN COD WITH SHRIMP & LEMON SAUCE

4 North Atlantic cod fillets, 8 - 10 ounces each
3 cups water
1 teaspoon salt
2 lemon slices
1 bay leaf
¼ teaspoon dried thyme
2 ⅔ cups precooked salad shrimp

Sauce Ingredients

1 cup Miracle Whip, or mayonnaise
2 tablespoons minced parsley
1 tablespoon lemon juice
1 tablespoon dehydrated minced onion
2 teaspoons Worcestershire sauce

In a large skillet bring the water, salt, lemon slice, bay leaf, and thyme mixture to a boil. Cook the fish fillets in the skillet at a medium boil until they flake easily with a fork, about 12-15 minutes.

While the fish is poaching mix the sauce ingredients in a bowl.

Thaw the precooked salad shrimp under tepid running water. Pat dry with paper towels.

Carefully place the cooked fillets on a broiler tray. Top each fillet with the seafood sauce and place about ⅔ cup shrimp on each fillet. Bake or broil the fish and shrimp until it is heated through and lightly browned on top.

Serves 4.

BAKED OR BROILED RAINBOW TROUT

4 boned, thawed, rainbow trout (10 ounces each)
6 tablespoons melted butter
½ teaspoon paprika
3 tablespoons lemon juice

Cut off and discard the heads of the trout. Open the trout to a flat position, skin side down, on a (lightly greased) metal broiling pan. Handle the pan carefully because the trout will be slippery. Brush the meat of the trout with the melted butter and squeeze the lemon juice over all. Sprinkle lightly with paprika.

Broil about 6 inches from flame for about 8-10 minutes. You can bake the trout at 400 degrees for 15 minutes also.

Serves 4.

STUFFED RAINBOW TROUT

Bake or broil rainbow trout as described above. Have crab imperial (or another seafood casserole recipe) precooked and preheated. When the trout is done place about ¾ cup of crab imperial down the center of the top surface of the cooked trout. Top the imperial with white sauce and a dash of paprika and place the fish back in the oven or under the broiler until the white sauce is hot.

EASY BATTER DIPPED HADDOCK

Use Golden Dipt brand English Style Fish & Chips batter mix and follow the package directions. A 10-ounce package of this easy to use batter will coat about 3 pounds of fish fillets.

You will experience the best results if you pat dry the thawed fish fillets before coating them.

If you are serving a large group and need to hold quantities of fried fish, hold them in a 275 to 300 degree oven for up to 15 minutes. The fish will hold its heat and remain crispy.

Staging your cut and dried fish, bowl of batter, and & deep fryer — assemble line style, will allow you to produce lots of fried fish at a brisk pace. Because the batter mix uses only cold water you can replenish your batter in a matter of seconds.

It is also a great batter for shrimp and scallops.

A sure way to tell when deep fried food is done is to watch and listen. When the food pieces float and move, and when the fryer begins a "hissing" noise, cook the food for 30 seconds longer and it will be done nicely.

After the oil cools, strain it through a fine sieve or cheese cloth. Seal the strained oil in a jar and refrigerate it for up to three months. Date and label the container holding the oil so that you'll know it should be used for frying fish.

Please try this, and other Golden Dipt brand coating products. They are user-friendly and have great flavor.

PAN FRIED HADDOCK

4 fillets of haddock (10 ounces each)
flour for dredging
Old Bay seasoning to dust each portion
vegetable oil for frying

Thaw haddock. Gently squeeze each fillet between your hands, over the sink, to remove excess moisture. Don't use so much pressure that you make the fillet dry inside. Blot the fillet with paper towels to dry the surface.

Dredge each fillet all over with flour while your skillet is heating over medium-high heat. Add enough vegetable oil to the skillet to reach half way up the sides of the fillets while frying. Test the oil for readiness before putting a whole fillet into the oil. Put a small piece or the tip of a piece of fish into the oil. If you get an immediate sizzling reaction the oil is ready.

Before placing the dredged fillets into the hot oil, dust them lightly with Old Bay seasoning. Fry the fish, turning to brown each side, for about 5 - 6 minutes per side. The fish is done when it flakes easily with a fork and it is pure white inside, about 12 to 15 minutes.

Serve on toast points with tartar sauce.

Serves 4.

BROILED ROCKFISH CATALINA

4 Pacific rockfish fillets
4 tablespoons butter
⅔ cup bottled Catalina salad dressing
seafood seasoning (optional)

Preheat the broiler.

Allow the butter to come to room temperature. Spread the butter evenly over the fish fillets. Place the fillets on a rimmed metal baking pan and put the pan about 4 to 6 inches under the broiler. Season to taste with seafood seasoning.

Broil the fillets for about 6 minutes if thawed and for about 10 minutes if frozen. Pull the pan from the broiler and spread the Catalina dressing over each piece of rockfish. Broil for 3 to 4 minutes longer.

Serves 4.

■ Pacific rockfish purchased locally usually contains some bones. Because of the way this fish flakes apart, in distinct chunks, the bones are readily apparent. Caution guests to watch for them as they cut the fish and also to chew each bite several times in the front of their mouths.

Please don't let a few bones deprive you of the pleasure of eating this fish. It has a very mild, almost sweet flavor, and has a nice firm texture.

MAKO SHARK STEAK AU POIVRE

4 Mako shark steaks (6 ounces each) skin removed
salt and 3 tablespoons coarsely ground pepper
½ cup clarified butter
2 to 3 tablespoons finely chopped shallots
⅓ cup brandy, plus more as needed
10 ounces whipping cream
¼ cup chicken stock

Pat shark steaks dry. Salt lightly. Arrange ground pepper on a plate. Dredge each steak in the pepper and shake off excess to leave a light coating.

Heat clarified butter (reserving a tablespoon or two) in a large skillet until hot. Sauté the fish until lightly browned on each side, 3 to 4 minutes per side. Transfer to warm platters, and keep warm.

Pour off all but about 1 tablespoon butter from the skillet. Add shallots and toss briefly. Carefully add the ⅓ cup brandy. Add the cream and chicken stock. Boil this mixture, stirring often, until reduced to a consistency that will lightly coat the back of a spoon. Taste and adjust seasonings. Use a little salt and/or pepper and a few drops of brandy. Pour sauce over the fish steaks to serve.

Serves 4.

■ Clarified butter, sometimes called drawn butter, is butter that has mild solids, and other impurities removed. To obtain clarified butter heat butter over medium heat until it begins to foam. Set the pan off the heat and allow it to cool for 15 minutes. The cooling butter will separate into 3 layers. Solids will be on the top and bottom, while the middle section will be clear. The middle section is the clarified butter. Gently ladle off and discard the top layer.

Slowly pour the middle section into another pan until the solids in the bottom begin to spill into the clarified butter container.

Clarified butter has a higher burning point, but less flavor than regular butter.

SALMON STEAKS - DILLED & GRILLED

6 salmon steaks or fillets (6 ounces each) thawed
½ cup butter melted
2 tablespoons lemon juice
2 teaspoons dill weed
dash salt
⅛ teaspoon ground black pepper

Combine the last 5 ingredients. Stir to blend. Baste the salmon on one side before placing that side down on a well greased grill rack over hot coals. Baste the top side of the fish. Grill for about 10 minutes cooking time per inch of thickness, measured at the thickest part. Turn the fish once. Baste often while cooking.

Serves 6.

■ Purchase a good quality French chef's knife. The French chef's knife (and its counterpart, the Oriental chef's knife) is the single most useful hand tool in any kitchen. Nothing will make you more efficient in the kitchen than mastering the techniques of this knife.

SESAME GRILLED FISH

4 fish fillets (8 ounces each)
4 tablespoons Kikkoman soy sauce
2 teaspoons sugar
3 tablespoons toasted, crushed sesame seeds
1 tablespoon sesame oil
1 clove garlic, minced
1 teaspoon ginger

Combine the latter six ingredients in a shallow dish to make a sauce. Turn each fillet (to coat each side) in the sauce and place on a greased broiler tray. Broil 6 inches from the heat until cooked throughout.

The fillets may be grilled over hot coals with equal success. Brush the fish fillets with the sauce as they grill to keep the meat moist.

Serves 4.

■ When grilling or broiling boneless fish fillets a good rule to establish the proper length of cooking time is that a fillet requires 10 minutes cooking for an inch of thickness. This applies when the grill or broiler is preheated.

■ A "grill topper" is a porcelain coated metal plate that sets on top of your gas or charcoal grill rack. It has a pattern of holes which allows the heat from the grill to reach the food. The holes are set close enough together that seafood and small vegetables will not fall through to the coals.

DILLED SALMON CAKES

1 can (15 ounces) salmon
½ cup chopped onion
2 tablespoons butter or margarine
⅔ cup dry bread crumbs
1 large beaten egg
¼ cup fresh minced parsley
1 teaspoon dried dill weed
1 teaspoon dry mustard
3 tablespoons butter or margarine

Drain the salmon reserving ¼ cup liquid from the can. Discard any bones or skin. Sauté the chopped onions in 2 tablespoons butter until tender, but not brown.

Place the reserved liquid in a bowl with ⅓ cup bread crumbs, the beaten egg, parsley, dill weed, mustard, sauted onions with pan drippings, and salmon. Mix well. Shape into 6 patties and roll them in the remaining ⅓ cup bread crumbs. Sauté over medium heat in melted butter until browned on both sides.

Serve open faced on toasted English muffins or toast points with asparagus spears and lemon cheese sauce.

This salmon mixture can be used as an appetizer when made into bite-sized nuggets.

Lemon Cheese Sauce

Melt 2½ tablespoons butter in a sauce pan. Blend in 2 tablespoons flour. Cook and stir over medium heat for about 5 minutes. Remove from the heat and add 1¼ cup milk. Stir and cook until thick and bubbly.

Stir a small amount of the hot sauce into 2 beaten egg yolks in a separate bowl. Return this mixture to the original sauce. Add ½ cup, shredded, sharp processed American cheese and 2 tablespoons (or to taste) lemon juice. Stir until nicely blended.

Serves 4 as an entree, 8 as appetizers.

SCALLOP BROCHETTES WITH GINGER-LIME SAUCE

1½ pounds sea scallops, each at least 1 inch in diameter
¼ cup melted butter or margarine
8 - 10 bamboo skewers

Ginger-lime Sauce

½ cup dry white wine
½ cup chicken broth
1 teaspoon fresh grated ginger
2 tablespoons minced shallot or onion
¼ teaspoon grated lime peel
½ cup whipping cream
¼ cup butter

Soak the bamboo skewers in hot water for about 30 minutes.

In a wide frying pan combine the white wine and the chicken broth. And the shallots, grated ginger, and grated lime peel. Bring the mixture to a boil and continue cooking, uncovered, at a boil until the mixture reduces by half.

Stir in the whipping cream and boil uncovered until the sauce reduces to about ¾ cup volume. Reduce the heat to medium and stir in the ¼ cup butter. The sauce is ready to serve when the butter is completely blended into the sauce.

Rinse the scallops under cold water and pat dry with paper towels. Thread the scallops on the skewers, piercing them horizontally (through their diameter) so that they lie flat. You can use two skewers set close together if the scallops are large enough.

Grill the scallops over hot coals until their meat is white throughout when cut to test. About 5 to 7 minutes. Baste the scallops with melted butter as they cook.

Ladle the ginger-lime sauce onto a serving platter or individual plates. Set the scallop kabobs on the sauce.

About four servings.

SHRIMP ALFREDO

40 medium raw shrimp - peeled, deveined, & butterflied
¼ cup cider vinegar
1 teaspoon salt
1 teaspoon dry mustard
2 teaspoons celery seed
⅔ teaspoon red cayenne pepper
2 teaspoons Old Bay seasoning
2 quarts water

Add the vinegar and seasonings to the water in a large pot and bring to a boil. Add the peeled shrimp to the boiling water and cook until they are pure white on the inside. Cooking time will be about 5 minutes. Drain the shrimp in a colander as soon as done. Hold at room temperature.

Cook 12 ounces of linguine in 3 quarts salted water for about 15 minutes. Stir frequently. Test for doneness by tasting periodically. Drain in a colander.

While linguine is cooking prepare Alfredo sauce:

¼ pound butter
½ cup grated parmesan cheese
⅓ cup heavy (whipping) cream
1 teaspoon fresh minced parsley
freshly grated black pepper to taste

In a large skillet melt the butter. Add the cheese, parsley, and the cream and stir to make a smooth sauce. It helps to crush any lumps in the parmesan cheese before adding the cheese to the skillet. Add the cooked shrimp to the Alfredo sauce and stir and cook until heated through.

Portion the linguine on four plates and divide the shrimp and sauce to pour on the linguine.

BOILED SHRIMP

5 pounds thawed raw shrimp, shell on
water to cover, 3-5 quarts, depending on size of the pot
2 tablespoons Old Bay seasoning
3 teaspoons salt
2 tablespoons dry mustard
2 tablespoons celery seed
1 tablespoon red cayenne pepper
1 cup cider vinegar
2 more tablespoons Old Bay for after cooking

In a large pot add the vinegar and seasonings listed above. (Reserve 2 tablespoons Old Bay) Cover and bring to a boil. Add the shrimp to the seasoned boiling water.

Stir the shrimp often as they cook. Stir from the bottom to rotate the shrimp around the pot. When the shrimp turn bright orange and when it appears about half the shrimp have curled in half, taste one of the largest shrimp in the batch. If it is done the whole batch is done.

Pour the shrimp in a large colander to drain. Sprinkle

the shrimp with the reserved Old Bay and gently stir with a wooden spoon. Allow the shrimp to rest a few minutes before serving.

SHRIMP SIZES (number of Shrimp per Pound)

Under 10	Largest available
Under 15	Next largest available
16/20	Jumbo
21/25	Extra large
26/30	Large
31/35	Medium large
36/40	Medium
40/50	Small
Over 50 count	Salad size

SHRIMP & FISH IN GARLIC SAUCE

¾ pound medium shrimp, peeled, deveined, & butterflied
¾ pound firm fleshed white fish, (monkfish, cod, haddock)
12 cloves garlic, roughly chopped
1 cup vegetable oil
½ stick butter, cut in 4 pieces
1 tablespoon minced fresh parsley
6 cups cooked rice

In a large skillet, sauté the garlic in medium hot oil until light brown. The garlic must not burn. When the garlic is light brown, quickly whisk in the 4 pieces of butter all at once. Quickly remove the skillet from the heat.

In a few minutes the garlic will become crisp. When crisp remove it with a slotted spoon. Reserve the oil and butter for sautéing the shrimp and fish.

Use about ¼ cup of the oil and butter to sauté the shrimp

and fish. Keep the seafood moving and add more oil/butter if needed.

The shrimp and fish are done when the flesh is pure white throughout. Cut a large shrimp in half to check. Cooking time over medium heat is about 6 minutes.

Serve over white rice. Sprinkle the browned garlic bits over the seafood and spritz with parsley. Use some of the seasoned oil/butter to moisten the rice.

Serves 4.

■ Spices can be evaluated by their aroma. If a container of an herb or spice has no aroma, it is time to throw it away, and buy a new small container to restock.

SHRIMP & HAM JAMBALAYA

1 tablespoon Old Bay seasoning
1 tablespoon dry mustard
1 tablespoon celery seed
1 teaspoon red pepper
1 tablespoon salt
1 cup cider vinegar
1 pound raw shrimp in the shell
4-6 cups water

Put all of the seasonings in a large pan with the water. Cover and bring to a boil. Put the shrimp in the pot and cook until curled in half. Cooking time will be about 5 minutes. Taste one of the larger shrimp. If it is done, the batch is done.

Drain the shrimp, reserving the water and seasonings. Allow the shrimp to cool. Peel and devein the shrimp.

Cook one cup long-grained rice according to package directions. Set aside.

1 cup chopped celery
1 medium onion, chopped
1 clove garlic, minced
2 tablespoons butter
1 - 16 ounce can whole tomatoes, crushed
1 - 6 ounce can tomato paste
⅓ cup water
1 teaspoon Worcestershire sauce
2 cups cubed, cooked, smoked ham
Bottled hot sauce

In a 3-quart sauce pan cook celery, onion, and garlic in butter until just tender. Stir in the undrained crushed tomatoes, tomato paste, water, and Worcestershire sauce. Bring to boiling. Reduce heat. Cover and simmer 15 minutes.

Stir cooked rice, shrimp, and smoked ham into tomato mixture. Season to taste with hot sauce. Cook, uncovered, until heated through, stirring occasionally.

Makes about 6 servings.

SHRIMP & HAM ETOUFÉ (AY-too-FAY)

To convert our Jambalaya to an Etoufé use tomato sauce in place of the tomato paste. Also add ¾ cup green peppers to the list of vegetables.

The Etoufé should be more moist than the Jambalaya and is served over hot cooked rice rather than with the rice mixed through the dish. To achieve the moistness required, add back to the cooked mixture of shrimp, ham, and vegetables, the liquid and seasonings in which you cooked the shrimp. An Etoufé is more like a stew than a soup.

Also an Etoufé benefits from cooking for a longer period of time in a covered vessel. Cook all the ingredients together remembering to omit the rice in an Etoufé. The rice is an accompaniment with an Etoufé and an ingredient in a Jambalaya.

SHRIMP MONTEREY

24-30 raw medium or large shrimp
4 tablespoons butter
2 tablespoons olive oil
4 cloves garlic minced
1 teaspoon dry red pepper flakes
⅓ cup white chablis wine
1½ tablespoons fresh minced parsley
four for dredging the shrimp
lemon garnish

Peel, devein, and butterfly the shrimp. Dredge them in flour.

Heat the butter and olive oil in a wide skillet over medium high heat. Add the red pepper flakes. Stir and cook for about a minute. Add the minced garlic and stir and cook for about a minute. Add the shrimp to the skillet and cook for about 6 minutes, stirring gently.

Add the parsley and white wine to the skillet. Stir and cook for a few minutes more.

Serve the shrimp with rice or pasta with the pan juices poured over all. Garnish with lemon.

Serves 4.

SHRIMP SCAMPI

1 pound, 26 to 30 count, raw shrimp
4 tablespoons butter
4 large cloves garlic
⅓ cup white Chablis wine
2 teaspoons fresh minced parsley

Thaw the shrimp if frozen. Peel devein, and butterfly the shrimp.

Mince the 4 cloves of garlic. Melt the 4 tablespoons butter in a large skillet, over low heat, and add the minced garlic. Stir and cook the butter and garlic for about a minute.

Turn the heat to medium-high and add the shrimp to the skillet. Toss or stir the shrimp to coat them with the garlic butter.

Add the ⅓ cup wine and the two teaspoons minced parsley to the skillet. Stir and cook for about 3 minutes, or until the shrimp are just cooked through.

Serve over rice or angel hair pasta as an entree.

Serves 3 to 4.

Or serve in a pineapple boat, garnished with fruit, as an appetizer. Makes 26 to 30 single appetizers.

POLYNESIAN SEAFOOD SCAMPI

(pictured on cover)

1 whole fresh pineapple per 2 guests
5 tablespoons butter
1¼ to 1½ pounds assorted white fleshed seafood
(shrimp, scallops, whitefish, lobster, crab or imitation crab)
½ cup Chablis wine
1 tablespoon minced garlic
2 tablespoons minced fresh parsley
Assorted fresh fruit of contrasting colors
(strawberries, kiwi, grapes, oranges, bananas, etc.)

Leaving the pineapple top attached to the body, cut through the body and top of the pineapple in a lengthwise manner to make two halves.

To hollow the pineapple halves into serving bowls, start about ½ inch, in, from the outer edge. Cut down and around the perimeter of the fruit without piercing the outer shell. Withdraw the knife and cut down either side of the core in the center. There will be one wedge of pineapple on either side of the core. Gently remove and save them. Now cut out the exposed core and discard it. Repeat process with other half of the pineapple.

Place the pineapple bowls on oblong platters, hollow side up. Place the pineapple wedges on the plate, and against each side of the round base of the pineapple bowl. Garnish the pineapple serving boat all around with colorful fruit.

For the seafood filling select your favorite white fleshed seafood varieties and sauté them in a skillet over medium-high heat in melted butter, minced garlic, and 1 tablespoon minced fresh parsley. After 6-7 minutes add a ½ cup Chablis wine to the garlic until done. The seafood is done when it is bright white throughout. Cut a larger piece in half to sight and taste test it. If it is done the rest is done.

Spoon the sautéd seafood into the pineapple boats. Pour the pan sauce over the seafood, dividing it equally between the two. Sprinkle a little more fresh parsley over each filled pineapple half and serve at once.

SEAFOOD STIR-FRY

1 cup thinly sliced cauliflower
1 cup thinly sliced carrots
1 cup fresh snow peas
1 cup miniature yellow corn
1 cup green onions - bias cut 1" pieces
1 pound seafood of choice
3 tablespoons peanut oil
¼ cup Kikkoman soy sauce
2 teaspoons sesame oil
chicken broth for added liquid (optional)
cornstarch and water for thickening (optional)

Perform the needed prep work on the vegetables and seafood. Arrange them on a counter or tray in the order in which you will put them in your pan. Dense textures first. Loose textured ingredients next. Precooked items last. The above recipe would arrange in this order using medium sized shrimp as the seafood. Carrots, cauliflower, green onions, shrimp, snow peas, and yellow corn.

Heat the wok or skillet over medium high heat. Add the oil and heat for just a few minutes. Swirl the hot oil to coat the pan. Add the carrots and stir to coat with oil. Cook 1 minute. Add the cauliflower and stir to coat with oil. Cook 1 minute. Add the onions and raw seafood. Stir to coat. If more oil is needed, clear a spot in the center of the pan and drizzle additional oil onto this spot slowly. You may add chicken broth instead of oil if you wish. Season now with Kikkoman soy sauce and sesame oil. Stir the ingredients to coat with the pan liquids.

Add the snow peas and miniature corn. Stir and cook

until the seafood is cooked through and the corn and snow peas reach serving temperature.

Serve your stir-fry over rice or very thin, quick cooking oriental noodles.

Serves 4.

MIXED SEAFOOD GRILL

½ pound medium sized shrimp
½ pound sea scallops
½ pound whitefish fillet (cubed 1 inch)
¼ pound butter
1 tablespoon white vinegar
2 teaspoons Old Bay seasoning
1½ teaspoons celery seed
2 tablespoons white Chablis wine

Melt the butter in a sauce pan. Add the vinegar, Old Bay, celery seed, and white wine. Stir to blend and remove from the heat.

Peel, devein, and butterfly the shrimp. Cut the fish fillets into 1 inch cubes. Place the shrimp, scallops, and fish in the seasoned butter and stir to coat. Allow the seafood to marinate for 30 minutes at room temperature, or for 2 hours (or more) in refrigeration.

Use a "grill topper" to cook the seafood over a hot grill for about 10 minutes. Stir often as the seafood cooks.

Serves 3.

SEAFOOD THERMIDOR

12 ounces langostinos
4 ounces crab meat
4 ounces bay or sea scallops
4 ½ tablespoons butter
3 tablespoons flour
1 cup light cream
¼ cup sauterne wine
¼ cup shredded Swiss cheese
3 tablespoons grated parmesan cheese
2 tablespoons minced green pepper
2 tablespoons minced onion

Melt 1½ tablespoons butter in a skillet. Sauté the scallops, green pepper, and onion until the scallops are pure white inside entirely. Set skillet off the heat.

In a sauce pan melt remaining 3 tablespoons butter; blend in flour with a whisk. Cook flour and butter roux for about 5 minutes over medium heat. Add light cream and stir with whisk. Raise heat to medium-high and continue stirring until sauce simmers and thickens.

Add wine and Swiss cheese. Stir until cheese melts and blends with sauce. Set aside about ½ cup of sauce.

Add langostinos, crab meat, scallops, green pepper, and onion to the sauce pan and gently stir to mix. Spoon seafood and sauce into small baking dishes. Top with some of the reserved sauce and sprinkle with parmesan cheese. Broil until hot and bubbly.

Makes 6 - 6 ounce servings.

TUNA ENCHILADAS

2 cups enchilada sauce
¾ cup sour cream
¼ teaspoon salt
¼ cup chopped green onion
¼ cup chopped green pepper
4 tablespoons chopped mild green chilies
1 cup chopped tomatoes
4 ounces (1 cup) shredded cheddar cheese
1 can (12½ ounces) chunk light tuna
8 flour tortillas
8 sliced pitted black olives

Preheat oven to 350 degrees. In a medium sized bowl combine 2 tablespoons enchilada sauce, ½ cup sour cream, and ¼ teaspoon salt. Cream together with a whisk. Next fold in the green onion, green pepper, chilies, ⅔ cup chopped tomatoes, ½ cup cheese, and the tuna (drained and flaked). Set aside.

In a small bowl, combine remaining enchilada sauce and remaining ¼ cup sour cream. Pour about a cup of this sauce mixture into a shallow baking dish and spread to cover evenly.

Warm the tortillas as per package directions. Fill each tortilla with ⅓ cup tuna mixture and place them seam side down (after rolling) in the baking dish. Pour remaining sauce over the tortillas. Sprinkle with the remaining cheddar cheese. Bake 25 - 30 minutes, or until hot and bubbly. Allow the tortillas to set up for about 5 minutes. Garnish with sliced black olives and remaining chopped tomatoes just before serving.

Serves 4.

LINGUINE ALFREDO

3 quarts water
2 teaspoons salt
1 tablespoon vegetable oil
½ pound linguine
¼ cup butter
½ cup half & half or whipping cream
½ cup grated parmesan cheese
additional parmesan cheese
fresh ground black pepper to taste
2 tablespoons minced fresh parsley

Bring water to a rapid boil in a large pot. Add salt and oil. Add the linguine and stir as the pasta softens. Cook the linguine until tender but firm (taste the pasta as it cooks). Drain the pasta in a colander. Save about 3 cups of the hot water as you drain the pasta. Place this water back in the original pot and place the colander holding the pasta over (not touching) the reserved hot water.

In a sauce pan or skillet melt the butter with the half & half or cream. Simmer a minute or two to thicken. Remove from the heat. Add the cooked linguine and the minced parsley to the sauce and toss gently to coat. Add the parmesan cheese and grated pepper and gently toss again.

Place pasta and sauce in a large serving dish and pass additional grated parmesan cheese in a shaker container.

Serve with salad and garlic bread.

Serves 4.

To accessorize this tasty pasta dish add a pound of 36/40 count, peeled and deveined, cooked shrimp. Boil the shrimp in a spicy brine of 3 quarts water, 1 teaspoon salt, ½ cup cider vinegar, 1 tablespoon celery seed, 1 tablespoon Old Bay, 1 tablespoon dry mustard, and 1 teaspoon red cayenne pepper.

ROLLED LASAGNA

10 lasagna noodles
8 cups seasoned tomato sauce
parmesan meatballs - optional
1 cup shredded mozzarella cheese
1 tablespoon minced parsley

Four Cheese Filling

1 tub (46 ounces) ricotta cheese
¾ cup finely grated mozzarella cheese
¾ cup finely grated provolone cheese
¾ cup finely grated parmesan cheese
½ cup sour cream
generous cracked pepper from pepper mill
½ teaspoon salt
1 teaspoon garlic powder
2 tablespoons minced fresh parsley

Mix all the cheese filling ingredients in a bowl. Cover and refrigerate for about an hour.

Boil the lasagna noodles in 3 quarts of salted water to which a few tablespoons of vegetable oil has been added. Cook them until they are just done. They should be a little firm to the bite, but in no way brittle or stiff. Cool the noodles under running water. Drain in a colander. Handle them very gently.

Dry each noodle with a paper towel. Lay them, one at a time, on the counter. Spread the cheese filling over the length of each noodle. It should cover side to side and be about ¼-inch thick.

Spread a thin layer of seasoned tomato sauce in a lightly greased shallow baking pan. Roll the lasagna noodles jelly roll style into single serving bundles. Set them in the baking pan, side by side. Pour a little tomato sauce over and around the lasagna rolls. Sauce should not be more than half way up the side of the lasagna rolls. Place meatballs, if used, around the pan. Bake at 350 degrees for about 20 minutes.

Remove the pan from the oven. Sprinkle a cup of shredded mozzarella cheese over the filled noodles. Return to the oven for 10 more minutes.

Sprinkle the dish with 1 tablespoon minced parsley just before bringing it to the table. Pass heated remaining sauce at the table.

Serves 8 to 10.

■ Your oven and broiler are hottest in the left, top, rear corner. They are the least hot in the right, bottom, front corner. Rotate foods to achieve even cooking and browning.

Test your oven with 2 potatoes of the same size. Place one in the top, left, rear corner, and the other in the right, front, bottom corner. Bake at 400 degrees. The potato in the top corner will be done about 10 minutes sooner than the one in the bottom corner.

MEXICAN LASAGNA

6-7 cups prepared chili
2 cups ricotta cheese
¾ cup sour cream
12 ounces cojack (or cheddar) cheese
4 cups salsa
3 cups enchilada sauce
12 lasagna noodles
1 teaspoon cumin
½ teaspoon garlic powder
3 tablespoons fresh minced parsley
green chilies to taste
salt & pepper

While you boil the lasagna noodles to a point of being just done, or el dente, mix the ricotta cheese and sour cream in a bowl. Season the mixture with 1 teaspoon cumin, ½ teaspoon garlic powder, 2 tablespoons fresh minced parsley, green chilies to taste, and salt and pepper. Stir to blend.

Grate the cojack cheese, coarsely, and separate it into 3 equal piles.

Drain and cool the lasagna noodles. Lightly oil a 13-inch x 9-inch baking pan. Place 3 cooked noodles in the bottom lengthwise. Spread a thin layer of the ricotta mixture on the noodles. Sprinkle the ricotta with some grated cojack cheese. Set aside about ½ cup grated cojack, now, for a final topping. Spread a layer of chili over the noodles and cheese. Drizzle about a cup of the enchilada sauce over the chili. Spoon a moderate amount of salsa over the enchilada sauce. (You may find it easiest to lay the cooked lasagna noodles on a flat counter while spreading them with the ricotta cheese mixture. They can then be placed in the pan.)

Repeat the layering process. Gently press down each layer as it is completed. Spread the remaining salsa over the top layer.

Cover the dish loosely with foil and bake at 350 degrees until the juices bubble around the edge, 30-40 minutes if starting with cold ingredients.

Before serving remove the foil and sprinkle the top layer of salsa with the reserved grated cojack cheese. Place it in the oven to allow the cheese to melt among the chopped salsa. Sprinkle the top with reserved parsley.

Serves 6.

PANCHO VILLA PIZZA

I've never made the same Mexican pizza twice. Results depend on leftovers, or what looks good on the grocery shelf that day. Use your imagination and have some fun making and eating these creative pizzas.

1 Boboli crust, 12 inches
¾ pound ground chuck
1 package commercial taco seasoning
¾ cup chopped green pepper
¾ cup chopped onion
3-4 cups salsa
2 cups cojack cheese
2 cups mozzarella cheese
sliced black olives

In a skillet, brown the ground beef. Add the chopped green peppers and onions at the beginning. Season the meat as it cooks with the package of taco seasoning. Spoon off excess fat after the mixture cooks.

Spread the cooked ground beef mixture over the Boboli crust. Then spread the salsa over the ground beef. Place the Boboli, on a sheet or pizza pan, in a preheated 350 degree oven for about 5 to 7 minutes.

Remove the pizza from the oven to spread the cheeses over the salsa and ground beef. Place the pizza back in the oven and cook until the ingredients are hot and bubbly. Dress the top with sliced black olives before serving.

Serves 4.

■ Use heat diffusers under pots and pans when preparing recipes that require medium to lengthy cooking times. The insulating capabilities of these inexpensive, double-layered, metal hot pads help prevent burning and scorching.

Vegetables/ Side Dishes

BUTTERED DILLED CARROTS

8 average sized carrots
2 teaspoons dried dill
3 tablespoons butter

Skin the carrots and trim the ends. Slice them on a 45 degree angle into even slices about ¼ inch thick.

In a sauce pan with enough water to cover the carrots add 1 teaspoon dill. Add the carrots to the seasoned water. Cover and bring to a boil. Cook until the carrots are crisp tender. Taste the carrots as they cook to tell when they are done properly. Drain the carrots in a colander.

Melt the butter in a small pan. Add 1 teaspoon dill to the melted butter and stir. Keep the butter over very low heat while carrots cook.

Combine the melted dilled butter and the cooked carrots into an oven-proof serving dish. With your hand or a plastic spatula scrape the dill from the colander used to drain the carrots into the serving dish. Stir.

This dish can be done a day ahead or hours ahead and reheated at meal time without any loss of flavor. You may need to add a little more butter.

Serves 5 - 6.

ITALIAN VEGETABLE TAGLIARE (julienne)

2 medium sized carrots - skinned
1 medium sized zucchini
1 medium sized yellow squash
1 medium sized red pepper
1 tablespoon minced parsley
4 tablespoons butter

Place the julienne blade in your food processor.

Cut the carrots in half and force them through the machine. Quarter the zucchini and yellow squash and force them through the processor. Core and seed the red pepper. Cut it in quarters and force it through the machine.

Melt the butter in a wide skillet and add the shredded vegetables. Sauté over medium high heat for 3 to 5 minutes or until just cooked. Sprinkle with the minced parsley and toss before serving.

Serves four.

ALAMO CORN CASSEROLE

2 cans (11 ounces) whole kernel corn - drained
⅓ cup finely chopped green peppers
⅓ cup finely chopped red bell peppers
⅓ cup finely chopped purple onion
4 ounces Mild Mexican Velveeta Cheese
½ teaspoon McCormick's Mexican Seasoning
1½ cups Kellogg's Corn Flake Crumbs
½ stick cold butter
½ pint whipping cream

In a buttered 1½ quart casserole dish pour one of the drained cans of corn. Combine the chopped red and green peppers, and the purple onion in a bowl. Mix half the contents of the bowl with the corn in the casserole dish.

Slice the cheese into thin strips. Layer half of the cheese over the corn. Sprinkle the cheese layer with ¼ teaspoon of the Mexican seasoning.

Now use ¾ cup of the corn flake crumbs to create another layer over the cheese and seasoning.

Slice the cold stick of butter into several thin squares. Place half of the butter pats on the corn flake crumbs.

Repeat the layer process again. Remember to season the second cheese layer with the Mexican seasoning. Pour the whipping cream around the edge of the casserole until it blends with the other ingredients.

Cover the dish and bake at 350 degrees for 30 minutes. Uncover and bake for 15 minutes more.

Serves 6 to 8.

MAQUE CHOUX
(MOCK shoo = "Smothered Corn")

8 medium ears fresh corn
1 medium onion, chopped (¾ cup)
¾ cup chopped green pepper
4 tablespoons butter
1 large tomato, cut up
¼ teaspoon salt
¼ teaspoon ground red pepper
¼ teaspoon ground black pepper
½ pound smoked sausage or kielbasa, sliced

Remove corn kernels from cobs with a sharp knife, cutting two thirds of the way to the cob. Then scrape the cob removing the rest of the corn and taking some of the pulp of the cobs. This should yield about four cups. Set aside.

In a four-quart sauce pan over medium heat cook onion and green pepper about five minutes or until tender.

Stir in corn, tomato, sliced sausage, salt, red pepper, and black pepper. Reduce to low heat. Cover and cook for twenty minutes or until corn is tender.

Serves 6 - 8.

■ Roast whole turkeys breast side down. Don't stuff the cavity. Instead put in ½ cup water and a few tablespoons of butter. Place the bird on a rack over broth or water and cook for 25 minutes per pound at 325 degrees. This upside down method yields very moist breast meat, and great flavor.

SHOE PEG CORN AU GRATIN

2 cans (10 ounces each) Green Giant shoe peg corn
4 ounces Velveeta processed cheese - sliced thin
½ stick cold butter - sliced thin
*24-30, 2-inch square saltine crackers **
1 ¾ cups milk

In a buttered 1½-quart casserole dish layer corn, sliced Velveeta, about 8 crumbled saltine crackers, and slices of butter. Repeat layers until about ¾ inch from the top of the dish. Be sure to top with crackers and butter.

Pour milk in casserole to reach just near the bottom of the top cracker layer.

Cook covered at 350 degrees for ½ hour. Uncover and cook for 15 minutes more. Rest 10 minutes before serving.

Serves 5-6.

* Substitute another flavor cracker to vary the taste of this dish. Ritz crackers take it in another pleasant direction.

SCALLOPED OYSTERS

1 quart oysters
¾ cup butter
48 - 2-inch saltine crackers - crumbled
⅓ cup finely chopped onion
1½ cup milk or cream
1 teaspoon salt
⅛ teaspoon pepper

Drain the oysters and reserve their liquid. Combine this liquid with the milk or cream to make 2 cups total. Set aside.

Melt 2-4 tablespoons of the butter. Toss about 1 cup of the saltine crumbs in the melted butter lightly. Set aside.

In a buttered 2-quart casserole layer about 1 cup unbuttered saltine crumbs on the bottom. Spread about 2 cups oysters over the crumbs. Next sprinkle one half of the chopped onions over the oysters, Pour 1 cup of the oyster liquid and milk over all. Dot with one half the remaining butter. Season with half the salt and pepper.

Repeat layering using remaining ingredients and salt and pepper. Pour remaining liquid over, and top with buttered saltine crumbs. Bake at 350 degrees for 20 to 25 minutes or until mixture is thoroughly heated.

Serves 6-8.

PEAS & LETTUCE WITH CREAM SAUCE

2 tablespoons butter
2 tablespoons flour
2 cups milk
1½ teaspoons sugar
¾ teaspoon salt
1 package (10 ounces) frozen peas
½ standard-sized head of iceberg lettuce

Allow the half head of lettuce to come to room temperature.

Melt 2 tablespoons butter in a sauce pan over medium-low heat. Whisk in 2 tablespoons flour and stir until well-blended. Cook the flour and butter over medium-low heat for 4 to 5 minutes. Set the sauce pan off the heat and allow the flour and butter to stop bubbling.

Add the 2 cups of milk all at once and mix briskly with a whisk. Return the pan to medium-high heat and bring slowly to a low boil, stirring as the sauce thickens. Turn the heat to medium after the sauce comes to a boil. Remove the sauce from the heat and season it with the salt and sugar. Taste it to see that is slightly sweet. Add sugar if necessary.

While you wait for the sauce to boil, heat about a ½ inch of water in another sauce pan. Place the peas in the boiling water. Allow them to heat and cook until the water just begins to boil again. Taste the peas to see that they are crisp tender. Drain them in a colander.

Shred the lettuce into short, thin, strips.

In a large bowl place a small handful of shredded lettuce for each guest to be served. Add about ⅔ cups of hot peas, per guest, to the lettuce. Now add enough of the sweetened white sauce to generously coat the peas and lettuce. Spoon the vegetables into individual serving dishes.

Garnish each serving with a sprinkling of paprika or salad supreme seasoning.

Serves 4.

BARBECUED POTATOES

3 cans (16 ounces each) small whole potatoes
6 tablespoons butter
McCormick's barbecue spice

Preheat oven to 350 degrees. As the oven warms melt the butter in a shallow baking pan. Do not allow the butter to brown.

As the butter melts drain the potatoes and pat dry with paper towels. Remove the baking pan from the oven and roll and stir the potatoes around the melted butter until they are well coated. Sprinkle them generously with the barbecue spice. Stir them again and add a little more barbecue spice to the areas that were missed.

Bake the potatoes, uncovered, for about 45 minutes, or until they develop a brown crust. Turn once while baking.

Serves 6.

TWICE BAKED POTATOES

4 large Idaho or Russet potatoes
1½ tablespoons butter or margarine
3 tablespoons creamy horseradish dressing
2 tablespoons sour cream
4 tablespoons creamy bacon salad dressing
1 teaspoon garlic powder
1½ tablespoons dried chopped chives
¼ teaspoon salt
¼ teaspoon pepper
paprika

Wash potatoes. Pierce the skin of each with a sharp instrument. Bake them unwrapped for 50 minutes in a preheated 400 degree oven. When done, allow the potatoes to cool to the point where you can handle them without causing discomfort.

Cut the potatoes in half lengthwise and scoop out the cooked potato pulp. Try not to damage the skins. Place the cooked potato pulp in a large mixing bowl. Add in any order the butter, horseradish dressing, sour cream, creamy bacon dressing, garlic powder, chives, and salt and pepper. Stir well to blend.

Taste and adjust seasonings.

Spoon the mixture back into the potato half skins. Over fill each potato half skin to make a more generous and eye appealing portion. Place in a shallow baking dish and sprinkle each with a little paprika. Cover loosely with foil and re-bake at 350 degrees for 20-25 minutes.

Makes 6 servings, ½ potato per serving.

PARSLEY BUTTERED MUSHROOM POTATOES

12 size B red potatoes
¼ pound butter
1½ tablespoons fresh minced parsley

Select well-rounded potatoes that are firm and free of blemishes. Twist an apple corer a little more than half way through the center of a potato. Leave the tool in place in the potato. At about the center of the potato, use a paring knife to cut down to the metal ring of the coring tool. Cut a complete circle around the potato, keeping the blade touching the tool inside. Slip the cut bottom portion down and over the handle of the corer. Use your thumb to push the "stem" of the mushroom potato free from the corner. Repeat with the rest of the potatoes. The cut bottom sections can be cooked and used for other purposes.

To cook the mushroom potatoes, steam them over water in a covered sauce pan fitted with a vegetable steamer rack for approximately 18 minutes. Test the potatoes for doneness with a toothpick or similar object. The potatoes are done when they offer little resistance to a probe with the tester. Be careful not to cook them to the fall-apart tender stage.

Melt the butter while the potatoes cook and stir in the minced parsley. Cook on low until the potatoes are ready to serve.

Place the potatoes, 3 on a plate, and drizzle them with parsley butter.

Serves 4.

FRIED RICE

There are many variations of fried rice. The recipe listed here has pleased many diners. If you experiment and add some of your favorite ingredients, I'm sure you will take this recipe to new heights.

Most Oriental chefs use day-old cooked rice when preparing fried rice.

PORK FRIED RICE

½ pound lean ground pork
½ cup each diced green onions, shredded carrot
1 teaspoon garlic powder
1 beaten egg
2½ cups cooked day old rice
2 tablespoons Kikkoman soy sauce
1 teaspoon sesame oil
1 cup chicken broth
¾ cup fresh or frozen peas

In a bowl combine ground pork, diced green onion, grated carrot, garlic powder, and beaten egg. Mix well by hand.

Fry pork mixture over medium heat until just done. Spoon off excess fat. Set the pork on a warm platter. Add peanut oil to the pan and heat. Add the cooked rice to the pan and stir and cook until heated through. Add the cooked pork, peas, and about half the chicken broth to the pan. Stir to mix well. Season the ingredients with the Kikkoman soy sauce and the sesame oil. Cook and stir until heated through. Taste and adjust seasoning and moisture. You may want to add more chicken broth. Serve as soon as you are happy with the flavor and texture.

Serves 4 to 6.

MEXICAN RICE

1 cup long grain rice
2½ cups water
2 teaspoons beef base
1 tablespoon taco seasoning
1 tablespoon butter

In a large sauce pan bring 2½ cups water to a rapid boil. Stir in 2 teaspoons beef seasoning base or beef bouillon, 1 tablespoon taco seasoning, and 1 tablespoon butter. Next add 1 cup of raw long grain rice. Allow to boil for 1 minute. Stir the contents. Cover the pan and set it over low heat so that the rice and broth are at a low simmer. Cook until the rice absorbs the mixture - about 20 minutes.

12 ounces ground chuck
½ cup each chopped green peppers, chopped red peppers
½ cup chopped onion
½ cup water
remainder of taco seasoning packet

While the rice is cooking brown 12 ounces of ground beef in a skillet. Add the chopped peppers and onions a few minutes before the beef is completely browned and cook them with the beef as it continues to brown. Tilt the skillet and skim off any excess fat. Return the skillet to the heat and add the remainder of the taco seasoning packet and the _ cup water. Cook and stir until the moisture reduces and the peppers and onion cook to crisp tender, about 10 minutes over medium heat.

When the rice and the ground beef mixture are both done, simply stir the two together in either the skillet or the pan holding the rice.

Recipe makes about 6 cups, a dozen 4-ounce servings.

YELLOW RICE

1 package yellow rice
2½ cups boiling water
2 tablespoons butter
1 teaspoon salt

Pour package of yellow rice into 2½ cups boiling water, 2 tablespoons butter, and 1 teaspoon salt. Cook for one minute at a high boil.

After one minute, cover the pan tightly. Turn the heat to very low. Cook over low heat for 25 minutes. Stir once about half way through.

Makes 5 - 4½ ounce servings.

To add some color to this delicious rice dish try adding one or more of the following ingredients about 5 minutes before serving: minced parsley, chopped green onion tops, chopped pimento, chopped red and/or green bell pepper, sliced green and/or black olives, chopped chives, or any other colorful addition you wish to use.

BAKED ONIONS

6 large yellow, white, or Vidalia onions
4 tablespoons butter
1½ tablespoons fresh minced parsley
salt

Leaving the skins attached, trim off just enough of the root end of the onions so that they will sit upright without rolling. Bake at 350 degrees in a greased baking pan for 45 minutes, or until they are tender when pierced.

Remove from oven and peel the skins away. Place on a warm platter. Spread the tops apart slightly and top with butter and minced parsley.

Serves 6.

STUFFED ONIONS

Boil six peeled onions in salted water for 10 minutes. Drain and allow to cool. Slice about ½ inch off the tops to form flat surfaces. Carefully remove centers leaving about ½-inch walls. Season onion shells with salt and pepper. Chop the removed onion and mix with cooked meat or poultry, cooked rice, bread stuffing, or any other mixture you may like. Pack the onion shells with the stuffing and place them in a baking dish. Butter the tops and sprinkle them with bread crumbs. Add broth or tomato juice to come halfway up the onions. Bake at 400 degrees until tops are browned, about 20-25 minutes.

Serves 6.

OLD FASHIONED SQUASH & CRANBERRIES

1 butternut squash, 2 pounds
2 eggs, beaten
⅓ cup melted butter
¼ cup brown sugar, firmly packed
1 teaspoon salt
freshly ground black pepper to taste
1½ cups raw cranberries, halved
salt

Peel the squash and cut into cubes. Cook squash in lightly salted water until tender. Drain well. Purée the squash in a food mill or food processor. You should end up with 4 cups.

Mix the puréed squash with the beaten eggs, melted butter, brown sugar, salt, ground pepper, and the cranberries. Put in a greased 1 q -quart casserole. Bake in a preheated 350 degree oven for 45 minutes. Cover loosely with foil if the top begins to get too dark.

Serves 6.

PARSLEY BUTTERED YAMS - JULIENNE

2 medium-sized yams
4 tablespoons butter
2 tablespoons fresh minced parsley
salt and pepper to taste

Select smooth skinned yams with no cuts or blemishes. They are easier to peel and are less likely to discolor.

Peel the yams and cut a thin slice off one side, lengthwise. This will make the yam (or any round fruit or vegetable) safer to handle as it will not roll out of control when pressured by a knife blade. Place the yam cut side down and begin cutting it into thin, long slices. About the time you have cut a little more than halfway across the yam, lay it on what is now the widest flat side. Finish cutting the yam into long thin strips.

Melt the butter in a wide skillet over medium-high heat. Add the strips of yams and stir and cook until the yams are lightly browned and a bit crisp. Sprinkle with minced parsley and salt and pepper. Serve immediately, or hold in a very low oven, spread on a cookie sheet.

Serves 3-4.

LEMON PEPPER ZUCCHINI

3 tablespoons butter
2 small-to-medium zucchini
1 small yellow squash
1 small red bell pepper
1½ teaspoons McCormick's Lemon & Pepper Seasoning Salt

Wash and dry the vegetables. Cut the zucchini and the yellow squash across their length into ¼-inch thick slices.

Core and seed the red pepper. Halve the pepper and cut out the white vertical seams running bottom to top. Slice about half the pepper into julienne strips.

Melt the butter in a skillet over medium heat. Add the pepper strips. Stir and cook for a few minutes.

Turn the heat to medium high and add the squash and zucchini. Stir or toss to coat with the butter. Sprinkle with half the Lemon Pepper Seasoning. Stir or toss to distribute. Add the rest of the seasoning. Stir again. Cook for about 5 minutes, stirring often, or until the zucchini is crisp tender

Serves 5 to 6 adults.

LEMON PEPPER ZUCCHINI - JULIENNE

3 small-to-medium zucchini
1 small purple onion
1 tablespoon McCormick's Lemon & Pepper Seasoning Salt
3 tablespoons butter

Slice the zucchini across their width into ¼ inch slices. Slice on an angle. Lay the slices flat on the counter top and cut them into ¼-inch strips.

Slice the purple onion into ¼-inch strips.

Place the onion and zucchini strips in a bowl. Season the vegetables with the lemon & pepper seasoning. Toss lightly in the bowl to distribute seasoning.

About 5 minutes before you are ready to serve them, sauté the zucchini and onion in the butter. Stir to coat, and cook until just crisp tender, about 5 minutes.

Serves 4-6.

VEGETABLE BROCHETTES WITH BUTTER SAUCE

This recipe (actually more of a technique) changes with every trip to the store. It just depends on what looks good in the produce department on that particular day. Typically, I'll use zucchini, yellow squash, red bell peppers, and baby carrots.

The key here is to balance the textures of the vegetables so that they all cook to the same texture on the grill. The densely textured carrots must be parboiled until near done. The cut squares of red bell peppers are also parboiled. The zucchini and yellow squash need not be precooked. Cut the zucchini a little thinner than the yellow squash.

Alternate the cut vegetables on skewers and baste them as they cook on the grill with ¼ pound (melted) butter seasoned with 1 teaspoon each of dried basil and dill weed.

Other candidates for the technique are purple onions cut in wedges, other colored peppers, small red potatoes, whole mushrooms, cherry tomatoes, and the miniature vegetables that are beginning to be displayed in supermarkets.

ITALIAN SEASONED VEGETABLE KABOBS

You may use any variety of summer vegetables to make these attractive kabobs. Select varieties featuring different colors and shapes to make the brochettes more interesting. I have chosen to use one piece or slice of the following vegetables to make each kabob.

zucchini - slice
red bell pepper - square cut
yellow squash - slice
green pepper - square cut
whole baby carrot
red bell pepper - square cut
whole brussel sprout
purple onion - wedge cut

The cut peppers, baby carrots, brussel sprouts, and purple onion should be parboiled or steamed to near doneness. Thread the vegetables on a skewer and brush them with the Italian butter dressing.

The kabobs may be baked, microwaved, broiled, or grilled until the zucchini is just tender and the other vegetables are heated through. Baste and turn the kabobs often as they cook.

Italian Butter Dressing

½ cup butter - melted
½ cup cider vinegar
2 tablespoons water
1 envelope Good Season's Italian Dressing Mix

In a small sauce pan melt the butter. Add the vinegar and water. Allow to cool for a few minutes and add the Good Season's Italian Dressing Mix. Stir to blend.

Desserts

OLD FASHIONED APPLE CRISP

1 cup flour
¾ cup sugar
pinch of salt
1 teaspoon baking powder
1 egg
4-5 cups peeled, cored, and sliced apples (golden delicious)
2 tablespoons brown sugar
⅓ cup butter, melted
1 teaspoon cinnamon-sugar mixture

Heat oven to 350 degrees.

Combine flour, sugar, salt, baking powder, and the egg. Crack the egg into the mixture without beating it. Use a fork and a mashing action to convert the flour and egg mixture into several lumps.

Butter a 1½ quart baking dish, or an 8-inch square pan and spread the apples in either pan. Sprinkle the apples with the brown sugar. Spread the flour mixture evenly over the sugared apples. Drizzle the melted butter over the flour topping and sprinkle with the cinnamon-sugar mixture.

Bake 35-40 minutes, or until the topping is nicely browned and the apples are tender.

Serves 6.

BANANAS FOSTER

2½ ripe bananas
2 tablespoons lemon juice
¼ cup brown sugar
3 tablespoons butter
¼ teaspoon cinnamon
2 tablespoons banana liqueur
¼ cup white rum
1 pint vanilla ice cream

Slice bananas in half lengthwise. Then cut them into 1½-inch lengths. Brush them with lemon juice. Melt sugar and butter in a wide skillet. Add bananas and sauté 1 minute. Sprinkle them with cinnamon.

Remove the skillet from the heat and add the liqueur and the rum. Immediately ignite and baste the bananas with the warm liquid until the flames burn our.

Divide the sauce and bananas over 4 servings of ice cream.

Serves 4.

CANTALOUPES & STRAWBERRIES IN WINE

3 cups fresh strawberries
3 small cantaloupes
1 cup sugar
1 cup Marsala wine

Wash and hull strawberries. Cut cantaloupes in half and remove the seeds. With a mellon baller hand tool, scoop out the fruit of the melons. Twist your wrist as you scoop out the melon to form melon balls. Save the cantaloupe shells.

Put the melon and strawberries into a large bowl. Add ½ cup sugar and 1 cup Marsala wine. Stir gently but thoroughly. Refrigerate several hours.

Sprinkle the cantaloupe shells with the remaining sugar and refrigerate them. When ready to serve fill the cantaloupe shells with the marinaded fruit. Spoon some of the marinade over the fruit in each shell. Serve chilled.

Serves 6.

PUMPKIN CAKE ROLL

3 eggs
1 cup granulated sugar
⅔ cup canned pumpkin
1 teaspoon lemon juice
¾ cup all-purpose flour
2 teaspoon ground cinnamon
1 teaspoon each baking powder, ground ginger
½ teaspoon ground nutmeg
1 cup chopped walnuts
1 cup sifted powdered sugar
2 packages (3 ounces each) cream cheese
¼ cup butter
½ teaspoon vanilla

In a large bowl beat eggs with an electric mixer on high speed for five minutes. Gradually beat in granulated sugar during that time. Stir in pumpkin and lemon juice.

In a small bowl stir together flour, cinnamon, baking powder, ginger, and nutmeg. Fold this mixture into egg, sugar, and pumpkin mixture.

Spread this batter in a greased 15 by 10 by 1-inch jelly roll pan. Sprinkle with chopped walnuts. Bake in a 375 degree oven for 15 minutes. Immediately invert cake onto a kitchen towel and sprinkle with powdered sugar. Roll up cake and towel jelly roll style starting from the short side. Cool completely. Unroll cake.

In a small bowl beat 1 cup sifted powdered sugar, cream cheese, butter, and vanilla with an electric mixer set on medium speed. Spread this mixture over cake and reroll. Cover and chill in refrigerator.

Cut into 1-inch slices to serve 10-12.

STRAWBERRY SHORTCAKE KABOBS

12 nicely rounded large strawberries
12 cake donut holes, coated with powdered sugar
1 container (16 ounces) Pillsbury Frosting Supreme, Vanilla
4 - 10-inch bamboo skewers
rainbow or chocolate sprinkles (optional)

Hull strawberries and wash them. Alternately skewer 3 strawberries and 3 donut holes on each skewer.

Place the vanilla frosting in a number 4 pastry bag fitted with a star tip. Pipe a wavy line of frosting on top of, and the entire length of, each strawberry kabob. The frosting works best when applied at room temperature.

Serves 4.

Use 4½-inch wooden sandwich picks to make appetizer-size strawberry kabobs. Skewer 1 strawberry and 1 donut hole on each pick. Pipe a little frosting over each appetizer.

Rainbow or chocolate sprinkles can be sprinkled over either style kabob.

OLD-FASHIONED STRAWBERRY SHORTCAKE

1 quart fresh ripe strawberries-halved
½ cup sugar
2 cups sifted flour
4 teaspoons baking powder
¾ teaspoon salt
6 tablespoons butter
¾ cup whole milk

Gently toss halved berries and sugar and refrigerate until well chilled.

Sift flour with baking powder and salt. Cut in butter. Add milk and mix well. Drop the mixture from a tablespoon onto a greased pan. Bake at 425 degrees for 15 minutes. Split the shortcakes with a fork. Layer the lower half with strawberries. Cover with top half of the shortcake and layer again with strawberries. Serve with milk, half & half, or heavy cream.

STRAWBERRY-MALLOW CREAM PIE

1 baked 8-inch pie shell
½ pound large marshmallows
½ cup heavy cream
1 quart hulled, washed, ripe strawberries
½ cup heavy cream - whipped

In a double boiler melt marshmallows with ½ cup cream. While the marshmallows are melting, set a few whole berries aside. Then halve the remaining berries and place them in the pie shell. When the marshmallow and cream mixture is melted, set the top boiler pan in a large bowl of ice water and beat the mixture until cold. Pour the mallow cream mixture over the berries in the pie shell. Refrigerate until chilled through.

When ready to serve, spread the pie with the whipped cream. Halve the reserved whole berries and place them around the top of the pie in decorative fashion.

Commentary

BRUNCH PLANNING

When planning a brunch one of the early decisions to make is how many guests to invite. In reaching this decision consider the size of your house minus the serving area you will need. Also, will this be a sit-down brunch or a more casual buffet brunch? Sit-down brunches limit numbers to table size and number of chairs.

When the style of brunch (sit down or buffet) has been selected and a guest list completed, you can proceed to the menu. If you have chosen to have a buffet brunch you will be wise to plan a menu that requires no use of dinner knives. It is much easier for your guests to handle one plate and one utensil. Use of a knife requires all sorts of machinations for the diner.

The most convenient table placement for buffets in terms of ease and speed of serving is a table set up so guests can pass down each side and serve themselves from the middle. When serving off a table that is set against the wall make sure there is plenty of room around the three exposed sides. Remember people leaving the serving table will pass others coming to the table. That requires room for two. You'll find it helpful to have electrical outlets near your serving table. Even one is ample if a plug-in electrical outlet strip is used.

Provide a logical serving sequence for your guests. Arrange food, china, and utensils in the following order. Napkin, dinner plate, hot dishes, cold dishes, salads, bread, and fork. If possible provide a space next to each serving bowl for the guest to set his plate down. Of course, make sure there is a serving utensil next to each serving dish. Provide two serving spoons at each serving dish if you use both sides of the table for serving. Provide the largest napkins available.

Try to make your table presentation attractive. Even if

you're using paper plates in a casual brunch setting, a few garnishes and flowers will help make your table attractive to the eye.

Traditionally, brunches are planned to be served between 10 A.M. and 3 P.M. If you plan a sit-down brunch, you'll have to be more specific about serving time. If you plan a buffet, have enough food on hand so a guest arriving late will still be able to fill a plate.

Don't be surprised if your brunch lasts into the late afternoon. Be prepared to serve a light supper that in no way duplicates your brunch menu. This is certainly a matter of choice on the part of the host/hostess. You may not care to continue, but it's best to plan for the possibility of your brunch turning into an evening party.

"GREAT DATE" MENU

Surprise your sweetheart with a romantic sunset picnic. Here are some ideas. I'll speak, in terms of gender, as the gentleman presenting the evening for the lady. However, ladies should feel free to reverse roles.

First, find the setting. One that works well is an elevated area with a view to the west. Look for accessible roof tops, hill tops, a clearing in the woods, etc. Check the almanac for the time the sun sets on a given day. Then visit your chosen area at sunset to get a feel for the place. Is the view worthwhile? Is it too windy? Too public? It pays to check it out.

Secondly, set your date. Explain to your sweetheart that you have an evening planned that will include some surprises. From that point on be very evasive about any details. Do give her a general idea about how to dress so that she is comfortable.

Assemble the needed equipment and amenities as your special evening draws near. Here's a suggested equipment list: blanket or table, chairs or stools, table cloth, portable gas or charcoal grill and appropriate fuel, grill hand tools, insulated cooler, plates, salad bowls, silverware, glasses, wine glasses, napkins, lighting (candelabra, oil lamp, battery lamp (avoid anything that may have an unpleasant aroma), portable cassette player with music tapes, aluminum foil, zip lock bags, garbage bag, matches or lighter, floral centerpiece, food and beverage, and perhaps a wrapped gift. Remember the salt and pepper.

Here's a suggested menu: Tossed salad of choice, dressing of choice, twice baked potatoes, sautéed mushrooms, garlic bread, lemon pepper zucchini, fillet mignon, cheesecake dessert, and Cabernet Sauvignon wine.

Make plans so that your sweetheart is out of the house for several hours on the day of your planned evening, or plan to do your prep work at another location. During this time you must make the twice baked potatoes and wrap them in foil. Sauté the mushrooms and wrap them in foil. Add extra butter before sealing. See that the pre-purchased cheesecake is adequately packaged for travel. Wrap the pre-purchased fillets in film wrap. Thick steaks take forever to cook. Purchase 1-inch fillets, or plan to butterfly them so that the cooking time on the grill totals 12-14 minutes.

Pack the cooler. Don't forget the wine. Ice down the contents and put the cooler in the trunk of the car along with the other equipment, tableware, and accessories.

Now all you have to do is take her to the dinner location 30 minutes before sunset. Play the music as you set up for her surprise dinner. As soon as your grill is up to cooking temperature set the steaks over the hottest area. Place the zucchini, potatoes, mushrooms, and bread (all still wrapped in foil) on the outer edges of the grill. Serve the salads while the steaks cook and the pre-cooked side dishes heat. Together, enjoy the good food, music, and wine as you watch the sunset.

HELPFUL ACCESSORY APPLIANCES

Two appliances we tend to forget are the slow cooker (crock pot) and the pressure cooker.

Much of what we've discussed has dealt with the need for speed. The crock pot is not fast, but the crock pot is easy. Load it in the morning. Set the temperature control on low. Go to work. Come home to a hot meal that's loaded with flavor.

For all-day cooking choose the crock pot that has a temperature control dial that reads off –low– hi. This model has electrical coils that wind around the entire height of the pot. This means even heat with no dangerous hot spots. The low-to-high settings are constant and safer than numerical temperature settings that require electrical surges to maintain specific heat levels.

You'll notice that even your most finicky eaters eat crock pot meals with unusual enthusiasm. It's the aroma. It tantalizes for hours, and the flavor never lets you down.

Remember all the stories touting grandma as such a great cook? Well it's quite possible her food did taste better than food cooked using modern methods. That's because grandma probably used her pressure cooker.

Please try this appliance. The pressure-cooking method seals in vitamins, minerals and flavor. And it is a fast cooking method. A pot roast is fall-apart tender in 35 minutes. Spare ribs cook in 20 minutes. Chicken falls from the bone in 20 minutes. Pork chops are fork tender in 10 minutes. That's microwave fast! This appliance is well-suited to today's life-style.

Many people, including myself, used to think that the pressure cooker was sure to blow the roof off the house. The new safety valves on modern cookers make it impossible to cause an explosion. If you make all the mistakes, short of leaving the cooker unattended for hours, the worst you will experience is a thin stream of steam escaping which depressurizes the pot. Read the instruction and you will do fine.

The basics of pressure cooking include: start with a clean pot and gasket; see that the steam vent hole is clear; note what foods the instructions tell you not to cook in the pressure cooker; add the proper amount of water called for in the recipe along with other ingredients; don't fill the pot over 3/4 full; seal the post so that the handles and safety latch are aligned; set the control on the steam vent; set the cooker over high or medium heat (recipe will designate) until the control jiggles; turn heat back until control jiggles 1-to-3 times per minute; begin timing recipe cook time; at end of cook time leave control in place while you cool the pot under cool running water or allow the cooker to cool naturally off of heat source (recipe will designate). That's about it.

Pressure cookers are not inexpensive to purchase. You might want to try a few recipes with a borrowed pot. Be sure to borrow the instructions also.

HOLIDAY PREP LIST

Here are some suggestions for things to do a day ahead and/or the morning of the holiday on which you get to prepare and serve the family feast.

A day ahead:

Make dips and spreads that will be used for appetizers. Cover tightly and refrigerate. The flavors of the ingredients will blend nicely during this time.

Go over your menu and make a list of ingredients. Make sure you have all the needed ingredients "in house".

Gravies can be made a day ahead and freshened with freshly made broth the next day. Be sure and taste the gravy first. The flavor may have gained strength. You may want to use plain water to improve texture.

Make salad dressings a day ahead.

Soups can be made a day in advance of serving. Restore texture after tasting just as described with gravy.

Firm-textured vegetables such as carrots or broccoli can be parboiled a day ahead. Be sure to undercook them. Drain immediately and refresh them with ice or cold water. Drain again and refrigerate.

Will you be using linen napkins and tablecloths? Now's the time to launder them if needed.

Locate written recipes to be used the next day.

Holiday morning:

Cover your table with a tablecloth and stack your dishes and flatware on one end. Fold the uncovered end of the tablecloth over and cover the service ware. Your table is partially set and will save you time later that you may want to put to better use in the kitchen.

Lay out serving dishes and utensils so you won't have to search for them close to serving time.

When I know I'm in for a lot of activity leading up to a large meal, I post the menu on Post-It notes at eye level near the stove. I check this list periodically and especially one half hour before serving time. Without it I'm likely to forget the dinner rolls or another lesser part of the meal.

Begin thawing foods that will be needed later in the day.

A few hours before mealtime cut your salad ingredients. Dry them and put them in your salad serving bowl. Cover with a damp paper towel and refrigerate. They'll stay fresh and crisp for hours.

Lay out pans, lids, and cooking utensils that you know you'll need. Stack them off to the side in the order you plan to use them.

Prepare garnishes ahead. If there's a danger that they'll lose color, brush them with lemon juice. Cover and refrigerate. List garnishes on your posted menu so you don't forget them.

If you intend to serve white wines chill them early in the day.

A cooler with ten pounds of ice could be very helpful and take some pressure off your refrigerator and/or ice maker.

Many casserole dishes can be assembled several hours in advance. Refrigerate them and bring them out later to reach room temperature before cooking. You can also refrigerate them right up to cooking time. Just add about ten minutes to their cooking time.

Crock pots can be helpful appliances when serving large meals. They're great for holding foods (soups, stuffings, sauces, etc.) for long periods of time.

Be sure and check the things you prepared yesterday. You don't want them forgotten because they became buried in the refrigerator. Before your company is scheduled to arrive go over your menu - appetizer(s), soup, salad, main dish, vegetables, and desserts. Do you have the cookware and service ware for each readily at hand and clean? If so it's simply a matter of applying the heat and serving in the proper order.

Happy Holidays

Index